How Far Is It To Bethlehem

The Plays and Poetry of Frances Chesterton

Compiled and Edited

by

Nancy Carpentier Brown

Foreword by Dale Ahlquist

For Michael

CONTENTS

ACKNOWLEDGMENTS

Many thanks to Aidan Mackey for all his research and assistance.
Aidan searched through many files and boxes and mailed me papers
direct from his Chesterton collection. I am honored to have his trust in
safe-keeping Frances's works.

Eternal gratitude to Denis Conlon for his immense help.
Denis has been collecting and compiling Chesterton material for much
longer than anyone, except perhaps Aidan. He sent me papers, copies and
encouragement, and continues to do so.

Thanks to Peter Floriani for his help with everything,
especially the heraldry, editing, prayers and encouragement.
Someone has to do the hard jobs.
Ora et Labora!

Additional thanks and gratitude to the Marion E. Wade Center for
awarding me the Clyde S. Kilby Research Grant 2011, which enabled this
project to be completed.

PROLOGUE

Otago Witness, Issue 2881, 2 June 1909, Page 73, author
unknown.

LADIES' GOSSIP

Mrs. G.K. Chesterton, like so many other clever wives of
distinguished husbands, runs the risk, perhaps, of lacking
that justice from the public which is her due. Yet, Mrs.
Chesterton has several titles to distinction; she is not only a
spirited and practiced debater, but she writes "occasional
verse" of a most rare and delicate beauty. She is likewise
keenly interested in social reform; she constantly presides at
"happy evenings" for the children of the slums, and is a
prominent supporter of the "Christian Socialist" ideals.

Frances Chesterton definitely runs the risk of not receiving the
justice due her as the gifted author of these inspiring plays and
poems. Over one hundred years after these words were so truthfully
written, we now seek to rectify that error. These works of Frances
Chesterton's—her plays, her "occasional verse", her essays—are for
the most part unknown. Much of Frances Chesterton's *life* is also
unknown. In order to learn more about her, both as a private person
as well as the public life she lived as the wife of Gilbert Keith
Chesterton, we must turn now to the work and the memories she
left behind.

I've researched Frances Chesterton's life for a few years in preparation to write her biography. But as I was collecting information, I discovered that Frances not only had published material in the past, but that it was long forgotten and her works lay in obscurity. It's time to shine a light on Frances Alice Blogg Chesterton. Before her biography is complete, I had wanted to assemble an edition of her works, both previously published and unpublished, in the hopes that these works will inspire in others an interest in the woman who was Chesterton.

If there is a common theme woven through this entire collection of her work, it is Christmas. Christmas inspired Frances, motivated her, and kept her from depression during the winter. The Infant in the Manger was her heart's desire, and she loved to describe His tiny feet, little hands, and small footsteps.

Frances's plays were written for Christmas Eve productions the Chestertons put on each year. They had a stage right in their house for such home entertainments they so richly enjoyed. My greatest hope is that they will be used again for such a purpose.

The essay was written before her marriage and sounds strikingly similar to G.K. Chesterton, so much so that one wonders if he inspired her words, or if she inspired his. In any case, we can see how they thought alike.

Many of the poems were written for Christmas cards, the missing years mean that either Gilbert wrote the poem, or in the later years that they are likely missing from any known collection. I hope to fill in the missing ones in years to come. The other poetry was found by chance in my search of small publications, or given to me by Aidan Mackey and Denis Conlon.

Also left to collect are Frances's letters. In a letter from a friend in July 1923, the friend compliments Frances on a sonnet that appeared in the paper. Which sonnet and what paper, we don't yet know.

In addition, Denis Conlon is aware that there was a small book published privately of Frances Chesterton's poetry. Most likely these copies were given away to friends. But thus far, a copy of this book of poetry has not been found.

Thanks are due Dale Ahlquist, Therese Warmus, Emily de Rotstein, John Peterson, Peter Floriani, and Gerry Bruen for their helpful advice as this project neared completion. Thank you to Ted Schluenderfritz for the cover art, and to Michael Brown for the cover design.

Now let us enjoy these works of Frances Chesterton's, and give her the justice due that she so richly deserves.

—N.C.B.

FOREWORD

The way that I got to know G.K. Chesterton was through his writing. The biographical information came later and only confirmed what I had already learned about him through his own words. Though he seldom talks about himself, he completely reveals who he is by talking about everything else. It seems that this is an entirely appropriate way for us to get to know his wife as well. Frances Chesterton, always in the huge shadow of the famous writer who was her husband, has remained a mystery to most of us. But thanks to Nancy Brown's incredible research, here is Frances in her own words. This is a breathtaking discovery of lost treasure.

We open this book and learn that Frances, like her soul-mate, is quotably profound: "There can be no liberal education when the eyes are closed or the ears sealed."

She pulls us in by her innate literary sense and command of the English language. No wonder Gilbert Keith Chesterton fell for her. Her poetry reveals a love of strong images accompanied by a love for good rhyme and alliteration, a precision of sight and sound:

> And though their bones be dust by dry winds fanned,
> Their great swords rust their glory in the sand,
> Their names a whisper in the void of time,
> Yet some faint echo of their faith sublime
> May reach us here. . .

She puts poetry into her plays. But in her plays, she does something even more splendid: through children, she makes one age connect to another, ages remote and unimaginable to each other. Her love of children is not bound by time. She cherishes and longs for children that are a thousand years old, but we see them through the costumes and swordplay and singing of "children of another day." She knows and they know what makes for a compelling story: danger and a happy ending. Neither is any good without the other. Frances gives the children what they want, just like any good woman would give them the treats they have pleaded for. The prigs can dismiss it as mere sentiment, the critics can sneer, but "beggarmen be better men than you." Frances was not looking for the critic's approval. She published these plays, she tells us, because she watched so many children performing them with great delight. I hope they find their way to the stage again.

All of Frances' poems are invitations. They call us to sit at her table, as she shares a reminiscence, considers the heavens, offers a cup of Christmas cheer. They are reverent and warm, filled with faith and good humor. There is even the subtle invitation to fight. In a Ballade to rival any of her husband's, Frances turns feminism on its ear and provides an insight that we do not get in any history books. It turns out that that the upper class women are quite unmoved by the sufferings of the suffragettes; they bring about a societal change not because they consider the vote a basic right but something thoughtless and irresistible: a fashionable idea.

Things move quickly from the ridiculous to sublime. We can imagine the two things were always jostling for space in the Chesterton household. Her written words indicate that Frances, like Gilbert, is equally at ease with the eternal and the ephemeral, the true home and the temporary one. We are invited to both places.

An invitation, of course, is a gift, and many of Frances' poems, like a finely-crafted embroidery, were given as gifts. There are several remarkable poems dedicated to Dorothy Collins, who was G.K. Chesterton's secretary for the last ten years of his life. We need no biography to tell us that this is a woman whom Frances loves as a daughter, a fellow traveler across the world and through life itself. Her poem recounting their journeys together, longing for "alien skies", is like looking through a photo album, with the odd wistfulness that comes from any happy memory.

One of the most precious pieces in this collection is a beautiful tribute that Frances penned in memory of her husband. It is a portrait in miniature, a keepsake in a locket. We see the man who always lifted his hand with a sign of welcome to everyone, when finally "the last guest entered . . . death. . ."

All the invitations are graceful and good. We are bidden to the warmth of a fireside, to the comfort of a home, to the peace that comes only in detachment from the world. But above all we are drawn to a spiritual resting place. The childless Frances Chesterton has a mystical connection to the Nativity. Even the goal of the Children's Crusade is not the site of the Holy Sepulcher, but Bethlehem. The empty tomb may be the hope of all mankind, but the manger is where we first meet God face-to-face and in the flesh. We enter through the Little Door and discover that Bethlehem is indeed not very far.

> —Dale Ahlquist, President of the American Chesterton Society

INTRODUCTION

This first essay was written by Frances and published in the *Parents Review* prior to her marriage. Frances was working for the Parents National Education Union under the guidance of Charlotte Mason, well known educational reformist of the late nineteenth and early twentieth century. Although she was hired as a secretary, Frances eventually went on to edit the *Parents Review*, give conference talks at their gatherings, and write essays like this for their publication.

I think this essay is a good introduction to Frances Chesterton and her mind, of which we have previously seen so little. The similarities to Chesterton are astonishing: they both loved Robert Louis Stevenson, they both valued the child as a person filled with wonder and delight, they both understood the importance of retaining that delight with life into adulthood.

Frances's reference to the "child curious innocent" is interesting in that she refers to Robert Louis Stevenson using a phrase we now often hear used to describe her husband, Gilbert.

The Open Road

by Frances Blogg
Originally published in *The Parents' Review*

A Monthly Magazine of Home-Training and Culture

Edited by Charlotte Mason.

Volume 11, 1900, pgs. 772-774

"To travel deliberately through one's ages, is to get the heart out of a liberal education."
R.L. Stevenson (Dedication of the Vol. Virginibus Puerisque)

In reading the essays and delightful letters of that "child curious innocent," as Henley so aptly called his friend R.L.S., one is struck more and more each time with the extraordinarily elemental personality of the man. We all know the way in which children give themselves up to the matter in hand, and the utter impossibility that grown-up people find of explaining to a child that the charm of jumping off the table into the arms of the patient nurse or sister ceases after the ninth or tenth time. "Again," or "more," is all the answer one receives. Stevenson, realizing that he possessed "the knowledge sure he should endure a child until he died," perhaps consciously cultivated this power of intentness on the matter under consideration—this getting to the heart of things which, he maintained, could only come by a full and fixed determination on the part of each human being to go through life in the spirit of the true explorer.

This one remark of Stevenson's, which I have quite at the head of this little paper, seems to me so full of meaning and of courage, that I have thought it worth while to try and piece together some of the many suggestive hints it seems to hold as to this very essential aspect of education.

No one who has read the now famous essays on "Child's Play," and the "Lantern Bearers," can doubt that Stevenson knew the child, that he possessed that primary qualification of a teacher, the comprehension of the other point of view. In no strict sense can we say that he ever tried to teach anything; but the fact remains, that his power of getting at the root of things made him, as it has made many great men and women before him, the true inspirer.

Unlike other teachers, though, Stevenson regarded education in the same exciting and adventurous spirit as he regarded all the other experiences of life; and it is this marvelous and courageous outlook upon existence that makes his work of such infinite value. "My mistress still the open road and the bright eyes of danger," was an exclamation forced from him from the point of view of physical existence, and this mistress of his, the open road and danger's bright eyes, led him nearer and nearer as time went on in the weary round of constant illness and weakness to the very elements of which his restricted life was as much composed as any fine sea-faring adventurous forefather of his own of the Elizabethan age.

Education, then, to him was a journey, full of the delights of wide landscape, fresh invigorating air, or alternate sunshine and shadow, the great wide road stretching infinitely before—leading to that heart of its own, the beat of which he so longed to hear. There can be no liberal education when the eyes are closed or the ears sealed. In this, as in everything else, the wayfarer must live to the full extent of his being.

Pitfalls he must find on that journey, blind paths perhaps, but through it all the philosophy of belief in the essential goodness, the actual significance of things created, the state of being "in love with life." This, I take it, was Stevenson's idea in curious opposition to the view of those many young decadents, his contemporaries, with regard to this poor worn-out old world. What sort of an existence can that be out of which we make no attempt to get the heart? To go through life, to experience childhood and youth, love and parenthood, middle age and old age, sorrow and death; to see nature, and to be acquainted with all that is best in art and literature, and not to know the meaning of these revelations, is not this to be truly uneducated? In such a case, we have not wrenched the heart from life, or compelled it to yield its secret—and how can we deal with these essentials if we know nothing but the outside appearances of things? And how are we to get this knowledge itself and its appearance? Stevenson's answer to the question is, "by travelling deliberately through one's ages."

In another essay ("Virginibus Puerisque 1.") he still further enlarges upon this idea. "We advance in years," he says, "somewhat in the manner of an invading army in a barren land; the age that we have reached, as the phrase goes, we but hold with an outpost, and still keep open our communications with the extreme rear and first beginnings of the march. There is our true base; that is not only the beginning but the perennial spring of our facilities; and Grandfather William can retire upon occasion into the green enchanted forest of his boyhood."

The conception of life as a journey is an old and much worn-out allegory, but, in Stevenson's hands, the conception becomes somewhat different. I fancy we all remember the delightful sensations of childhood produced by the knowledge that a journey was about to be undertaken. The true meaning of packing, of ticket taking, of stations and porters, has perhaps never dawned upon us since, but, to the child, there is no doubt of the extraordinary significance of each act in connection with the exciting event. We can all believe that a child really lives through each moment of that enchanting time and is unendingly surprised at the want of interest shown by the grown-ups.

And this journey through life Stevenson conceived in much the same spirit; it was, to him at least, a deliberate conscious undertaking on the part of the individual, and there seems to have been one possibility in his mind for the supposition that this journey was being driven forward by some unknown power towards some infinitely distant goal.

Let us face facts, he appears to say. At present I am young, but I shall soon be middle-aged, and even old—let me at least understand each step of the way, miss nothing of the sights and sounds around; let me frequently look back at the portion of the road already traversed, that I may still, at all events, recognize that which was once so extraordinarily familiar; let me look forward, too, sometimes, that the road may not astonish me with its length or apparent difficulties.

This surely is deliberate travel. To accept each stage as it comes, to be unseparated by any barrier from the past, to be wholly at one with the present, and to hold out a hand of welcome to the future. Those people who possess this power of being in touch with existence at any given point are they of whom the Greeks wrote long ago, "those whom the gods love die young;" to them, at least, there is no getting old. Each step is but the completion of the one that went before.

And is it not possible that we may inspire children with a little measure, at least, of this brave and deliberate spirit? Can we not do something towards helping them to look upon life with that sense of adventure and anticipation in which they regard their childish journeys?

The difficulties with respect to education seem to become greater the nearer we grow to any conception of the real meaning and importance of the word. And yet "pluck" in this, as in most other things, seems to be the means by which alone we even dare to attempt to educate. There seems to be, in many children of the present day, a lack of the power of "grip," and, instead, a peculiar faculty for wandering all round a subject without getting to the essential meaning of it, not only with regard to the problem of learning, but in dealing with the actualities of existence which surround the child on all sides—too little idea of the meaning of words, of the significance of actions. It is, I think, because we grow accustomed to doing every-day things without ever, or at any rate very seldom, realizing the spiritual significance of the acts, that this dulling of the perceptions arises. We believe in the formation of habits of order, cleanliness and regularity. Is there not sometimes a danger that the very ease with which the children have learnt to be orderly, clean and punctual may lead them to think these things of no weight, or, rather, that these trivial acts have no special or more inward significance? After all, why should we grow used to getting up every morning, or washing our hands before meals? It surely would not matter if we reminded ourselves and the children, now and then, that these little acts which we repeat so lightly day by day, are, after all, ceremonies of very real meaning, and that to "grow used" to the symbolic actions of getting up and washing is akin to that grudging spirit that takes for granted all the wonders of creation.

In order that the flavour and scent of existence may not be lost, we must have within ourselves some consciousness of this impelling power that may lead us to travel deliberately through our ages, realizing that the most wonderful adventures are not those which we go forth to seek.

We shall then, perhaps, have some glimmering idea of what Stevenson himself meant when he said, "whether the past day was wise or foolish, to-morrow's travel will carry me body and mind into some different parish of the infinite." The conception of ourselves and our children as citizens of the "parish of the infinite" is undoubtedly one that must give us pause.

PART ONE: PLAYS

Frances Chesterton's Original Preface to *The Children's Crusade, Sir Cleges, and The Christmas Gift.*

Original copyright 1924. Samuel French Co.

These little plays make no pretence to any historical or literary value. They merely serve as a text or background for the exercise of that ingenuity and love of pageantry and even rhetoric which is the common heritage of all children.

The only excuse the author has to offer for their publication is that they were immensely enjoyed by the children who took part in them—not the least part of the enjoyment being the making of clothes, painting of heraldic shields, armor, royal robes, etc. The scenery can be of the simplest description—in fact curtains only are quite sufficient. The author has had so many applications for leave to produce the plays that it seemed well that they should be printed and easily available for others who may find it difficult to obtain plays really suited to children of varying ages.

FRANCES CHESTERTON

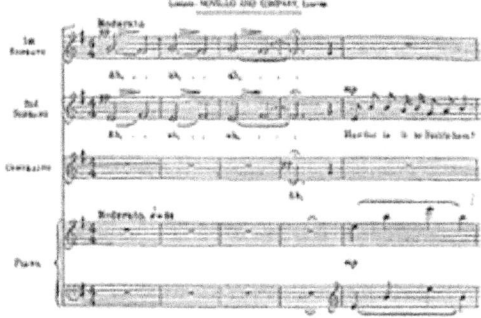

The Children's Crusade

In Four Scenes

Scene I   Rahire's castle in England

Scene II   An oasis in a desert

Scene III   On the road to Bethlehem

Scene IV   The Homage of the Crusaders

DRAMATIS PERSONAE

Prologue

Rahire   (Ra-HARE) Crusader and Minstrel

Blondel   Servant of Coeur de Lion

Lady Blanche   Rahire's Wife

Guy   \

Hugh   Rahire and Lady Blanche's Children

Jeanne   /

Radgund   A Nurse

Achmed \

Elkan   Moorish Pirates

Maralto /

A Woman of Bethlehem

Herald

Page

Crusaders: Peter the Hermit

             Godfrey de Bouillon

             Richard Coeur de Lion

             Berengaria

             Knight Templar

             Philip, King of France

             Tancred

Epilogue

Notes: "The Crusader's Carol" is also called "The Shepherds Found Thee by Night" and can be found through your library by requesting: The Musical Times, Volume 64, No. 970, in the extra supplement, December 1, 1923 (found on internet at http://www.jstor.org/pss/913723 where you can also buy it on line). The music of Blondel and Rahire's songs were written by Frances

Chesterton, and in those days, one could write her and she'd send you copies of her sheet music. In our time, so far, those sheets have not been found. Until they are, you are encouraged to compose your own music to fit the poems included in this book.

Peter Floriani has noted that *The Crusader's Carol*, aka *The Shepherd's Found Thee by Night*, can be sung fairly well to "I Saw Three Ships" if you alter the emphasis a little bit.

Please see Appendix for ideas about how to make the crusaders' shields, as the Herald announces in the fourth scene. —Ed.

PROLOGUE

In simpler days than these men dreamed one dream

Of some vast army marching to redeem

From heathen hands the sepulcher of Christ,

With faith ablaze by chivalry enticed,

They wandered forth from earth's four corners far,

Following as the kings of old that star

That ever beckons souls to the unknown,

Because man cannot live by bread alone.

And though their bones be dust by dry winds fanned,

Their great swords rust their glory in the sand,

Their names a whisper in the void of time,

Yet some faint echo of their faith sublime

May reach us here. And so we children bold

Tell you a tale new-fashioned from the old.

Look with indulgent eyes upon our play;

History there's none, nothing save names that may

Sound with an ancient charm about your ears

And so pass muster. Hope shall belie our fears

Tonight. We trust in your known kindness, friends,

Now as our story starts until it ends.

THE CHILDREN'S CRUSADE

Scene I—A room in Rahire's castle, simply furnished, weapons on the walls and in corners, a window, Nurse Radgund spinning in background. Children playing with hobby horse.

Guy   I wish I were a real grown man

              Like to our father; for he can

              Draw the longest arrow in the castle bow,

              And with his sword can slay the fiercest foe.

Hugh   And he can ride the wildest swiftest horse,

              And chase the boar upon the hardest course,

              And fight the Moor——

Jeanne   And sing such lovely songs

              Of knights and ladies; all the city throngs

              When father sings——

Nurse   Poor things, poor things, 'tis well they can forget

He lives in some foul dungeon, or more fearful yet,

Dead in a desert or drownèd in the sea,

Rahire! my master, lord of minstrelsy.

Gay troubadour, friend of the great Blondel,

Like him a poet of lay, rondeau, and rondel.

Blondel a wanderer too, seeking his king,

Seeking forever and as he seeks he sings.

Guy   I've heard Blondel sing; it went like this

(Hums Blondel's air.)

(Triolet.)

"Sorrow fills my heart,

Oh Richard, oh my King,

That you and I did part

Sorrow fills my heart.

But Blondel with his art

Will strive awhile to sing

Though sorrow fills his heart,

Oh Richard, oh my King!"

Jeanne   Yes, that's Blondel's song.

Hugh   I am a knight. Just see how I can tilt.

            Sir, you're unseated and your blood is spilt.

(On hobby horse tilts at GUY and knocks him down.)

Jeanne   And I'm a lady fair, I'll bind his wounds *(she does so)*.

            He is not badly hurt, he only swoons.

            (Enter LADY BLANCHE, distressed.)

Lady Blanche

            Children, children dear, my little maid,

            My lovely boys, ah me, I am afraid

            To hurt you so, yet would you hear the truth

            From other lips less fit than mine, forsooth!

            The great crusade that left this happy shore

            Is broken, lost, defeated, nevermore

            To march with banners flying in the breeze

            And trumpets sounding, when like summer trees

            The brave plumes of the mighty warriors toss

            Beneath the standard of the Holy Cross.

Your father lies a captive or a slave

In cruel hands, with all the noble brave

Who sought to see Jerusalem's holy hills.

Nurse   Alas! Alas! yet is it as God wills?

Lady Blanche

Yea, yea, Radgund—pray I may feel it so,

I should be brave in this my hour of woe.

Hugh   (*emphatically*) Our father is not dead—he will return!

Guy   Mother, I'm sure he will—and I will learn

To fight and ride like him and like him sing,

Till all the valleys laugh and all the mountains ring.

Lady Blanche

Brave lads! You are indeed your father's sons,

You comfort my poor heart that sadly runs

its tale of years.

Nurse   Ah me! My Lord Rahire.

What can poor women do? How shall they bear

The care of lands, castle and children too

In these rough times, there's naught that they can do.

Lady Blanche

They must do men's work, Radgund,

when men are gone

Forget their parts, forget they are women born.

(Embracing children.)

Now must I leave you, much must indeed be done

To make all safe before the set of sun,

Be quiet and gentle, be each a little knight,

Defend your sister dear—sweethearts, goodnight.

(Goes out weeping.)

Nurse   She has a royal air and wears her sorrow

How like a queen—but ah, I fear the morrow.

I will follow—she loves old Radgund well,

But how she loves Rahire—no tongue of mine can tell.

(Exit Radgund.)

Hugh   Jeanne, do not cry. Father will soon be here.

Guy   Oh, I wish I were a man. I'd find him, never fear.

            Captive or slave I'd ride and set him free,

            Bring him safe back to home, where he should be.

Hugh   Guy! what's that you said? "You'd set him free"?

            Well surely it might be so—just you and me

            Go forth in arms and find the holy land,

            Search for our father, and maybe we shall stand

            Within the holy gates. Jerusalem—hail!

(Seizes and waves a sword.)

Guy   Join the Crusade? and what if we should fail?

Hugh   Then must we die as many a one has done,

            Children like us, but heroes every one—

            Come, let us arm; here, take ahold this shield.

            It ought to serve upon the battle field.

Guy   And here's my sword, it is a trusty blade.

          With this in hand, I'll never be afraid.

Hugh   Head-pieces too, and greaves we have to wear;

          Here, buckle this—a breast-plate I would bear,

          But it's too big—the cross on your left arm;

          When we have that, nothing can do us harm.

Jeanne   But you've forgotten me. I must come too;

          You boys must have some woman to look after you,

          Some one must clean, and mend and pray and cook.

Guy   Be not so foolish, Jeanne—dear heart—now look,

          A maid cannot wear armor nor a sword.

Jeanne   Oh brothers, let me come and I may find

          The little Lord in Bethlehem…I'll mind

          Whatever you say. See here's a tiny lance (*takes one*),

          Just right for me….Now let them all advance!

(She lunges.)

Some day some greater Jeanne in arms will ride

(with lance uplifted)

And think of little Jeanne in all her pride.

Hugh, Guy, brothers, I pray you let me go

With you. I'm armed and ready, and I know

I'll find our father, for 'tis I can sing

His songs, like this. *(Sings an air.)*

You're wavering. Let me come.

Guy   Sister, the way is dark and rough,

Fit for boys and men—But there, enough,

Perhaps it were better so, we will not part,

We three together, so let it be, sweetheart.

Hugh   We are prepared and ready. Let us kneel here

And pray the saints to keep us safe from fear.

ALL TOGETHER *(kneeling, bowed heads over the sword hilts.)*

St. Michael and All Angels now give heed,

Be with thy children in their hour of need.

(Curtain.)

Scene II.

In the desert

(Enter children, ragged, weary, footsore.)

Guy   Let us lie here a little while and sleep.

Heap up the sand just here, Jeanne can creep

Under my arm. And this cloak I can fold

Just around her so—it will keep off the cold.

Hugh   I am weary. I think I'm well nigh dead.

We've naught to eat, not even a bit of bread.

My leg hurts so—truth, I can do no more.

Guy   Oh, Hugh, why did we come, my heart is sore.

We're utterly undone—we're all alone

In this vast place, and every hope is gone.

Jeanne   But we'll find Father, he is not very far;

Perhaps just beyond those hills where people are.

But I'm so tired—I'll have a little rest

Then I'll go on…

Hugh   Indeed, that will be best.

Guy *(to Hugh)* And you shall sleep, too—I will be on guard.

(They settle down to sleep.)

Guy   St. Michael help me now to keep my ward.

(Guy walks up and down like a sentinel.)

I am the oldest and I must be brave,

But oh! I am hungry…How I crave

For bread…We are alone—we have no friends,

Perhaps we must die—and thus our journey ends.

What's that?

(A noise behind. Elkan and Maralto break through.)

Elkan　　　　*(Seizing Guy)*

See here a very gallant Christian knight!

Maralto　　　And here's another, and in what a plight!

(Rudely shaking him.)

Maralto　　　And by the Prophet's beard—a little maid.

Stragglers they, wanderers from that mad crusade

Of children trained and armed, who thought

To conquer Saladin by force, and brought

Nothing but death, disease, and slavery.

Curse them, Christian dogs, and let them die.

Guy   Oh, spare us, spare us—we are very young.

We cannot fight, our life is but begun.

Hugh   Oh, do not slay us—we are so far away

From all who love us, oh, I pray, I pray.

Jeanne   We must find our father. Then I know

He will not let you hurt us, so please go.

(Enter Achmed.)

(Elkan and Maralto salaam.)

Achmed   What's this, some Christian children wandering here?

Well, what's to do? Maralto, Elkan, bear

Them as captives, by tomorrow's sun,

Unto my tent—white slaves every one.

(Children are chained.)

Achmed	The boys can serve upon our galley ships,
	The girl to a harem…See the red sun dips
	Low behind the walls of sand…Let them sleep
	Here on the ground till dawn. Here's a heap
	Of sacks for covering. Look you, guard them well.
	The Prophet bless you.…brothers, fare you well.

(Children lie on ground, covered with sacking, occasional sobs.)

Jeanne	I'm frightened, brother, oh, what shall I do?
Guy	Hush, sweetheart, hush. I'm here to comfort you.
Hugh	I'd rather die than live with them a slave.
	Let them slay us here and bury us in one grave.
	There is no hope—

Elkan	Cease whispering there…Maralto, watch awhile,
	For I must sleep. I'm tired. Achmed may smile,
	He knows not weariness nor pain, but I
	Burn with the high day's heat and longingly
	Look for deep sleep and the cool airs of night.

(Sleeps. Maralto watches.)

Maralto   I'll do the same.

The children are tied fast, blest be the Holy Name.

(Blondel, creeping cautiously.)

Blondel   Those two are pirates, but I heard a voice,

And English words…I think no one of choice

Would lie here in the dark with evil men.

I'll sing my song (*hums*) and then

They'll know that help is nigh.

(Blondel sings his song.)

Jeanne (*Starting up*)

Blondel's song! (*She repeats it.*)

Brothers, he is here…Blondel—Blondel….Come,

Oh, lift me in your arms and take me home.

Blondel   What? Rahire's maid, a captive and in chains?

His boys! While reason, strength and love remains,

They're for his children. Oh, Rahire, my friend,

These little ones are yours, and heaven send

That I may save them. See, here is bread.

Eat but a little, but you must be fed.

Follow where I lead—softly—look not round,

Take hold my hands and make not any sound.

The cruel men might wake and we be slain.

God grant they sleep on and never wake again.

Jeanne   We came to find our father. Blondel, where is he?

Blondel   Alas, I know not—a wanderer—but maybe

We shall find him yet. Courage, children dear,

We'll go to Bethlehem—a woman there

Will care for you—for that the Holy Child

Born in a stable there, in winter wild,

And Mary Queen a refuge there did find

From snow and cold and from the bitter wind.

'Tis but a two days' march—and I believe

We'll reach the holy place on Christmas Eve.

(Curtain.)

Scene III

On the road to Bethlehem

(Enter Rahire.)

(Sings.)

Rahire   The great sun is aflame,

The clouds ride high in air,

But there is none to sing

Save poor Rahire, Rahire.

The stony way is rough

To him who needs must fare

Upon the desert track

Like poor Rahire, Rahire.

Dangers on every side,

And cruel men to fear.

And he must go alone,

Alas, Rahire, Rahire.

And there are thoughts to hide,

But thoughts that he must bear

Lest he, a grown man, weep.

Ah, sad Rahire, Rahire.

Yet shall he sing his song,

A wandering minstrel here,

Whose life is well-nigh done.

Ah, poor Rahire, Rahire.

Rahire   It seems I have not lost my trick of verse,

Though I stand here in rags and die of thirst,

Mayhap of hunger, pain, or cold, or heat.

Yet there's life here, how my pulses beat

With mad desire to live, to see again

My lovely Blanche, my boys, my little Jeanne,

My friends and comrades, the deep woods of home,

The hills and valleys and the great sea's foam,

To hear the bells of my own village call

Across the fields, to sit in mine own hall

And give good cheer to rich men and to poor.

My heart will break with fear that nevermore

These dear things shall be mine; and now I seek

To join my friends in arms upon the way

That leads to Bethlehem, yea, even today,

This holy day (for it is Christmas Eve)

Mine eyes might see the plumes and shining greave

Of Godfrey, or of Richard, and many another

Hero Crusader, and my knightly brother.

I am pursued, I fear the pirate crew

Achmed and his men, lawless nomads, who

Capture children and turn them into slaves,

And murder men and give a nameless grave

To those who bear on shield an honored name,

Whose story they would thus-wise end in shame.

After long months I have escaped at last,

And liberty is sweet; I hold it fast.

For safety as a Moslem I must pass,

Slink like an adder through the sand and grass.

This cape will disguise me close enough,

God knows, my face is dark and tanned and rough.

By chance I found it lying on the ground

When I escaped their hands. I'll throw it round

Me, thus. (*Puts on hooded cape.*) What's that? footsteps, I

must hide.

(*Enter Blondel with children.*)

Jeanne   Oh Blondel, Blondel, are we getting near

To Bethlehem?

Blondel   We are nearly there.

Jeanne   Then I shall see my father very soon.

Blondel   We shall be there before the silver moon

Is risen in the sky.

Guy   I feel quite big.

If Achmed came along I'd stick him like a pig.

Hugh   I'd fight him too, and go at him like this,

Run at him with my sword and with my fist,

I'd hit him till he cried to me to stop.

And I'd not stop till I stood on top

Of him, my foot upon his neck—I long to fight.

(Rahire moves forward.)

Hugh   To strike one blow for father and the right.

Guy   A Moor! a pirate, at him, let him lie

In the dust.

Hugh   We're Christian boys, curse him, die he must.

(Both rush at him.)

Rahire   Mercy, mercy! *(Breaks away from them and throws off disguise.)*

Am I indeed awake?

My children here, my Jeanne? For pity's sake,

Ah, tell me if I dream; it is too sweet

For truth. What angel sent you here to meet

	Your father?
Jeanne	No angel, father, Blondel found us lost.
Hugh	Weary and hungry, thirsty, dead almost,
	In the desert, captured there by cruel men.
Jeanne	He said he knew we'd all find home again.
Rahire	Blondel, my friend, oh 'tis a joy indeed
	To greet you, savior in the hour of need.
	How can I thank you, how?
Blondel	No thanks are due.
	I am your friend, your children are but you
	In another form, though every whit as dear.
Rahire	Yet understand I not how you came here.
Guy	We came, we three, across the raging main,
	Across the mountains and across the plain,
	By monstrous towns and many a village fair,
	And last of all unto this desert bare.
Hugh	To find our father, for our mother grieved
	For him, and I think that she believed
	Him dead.
Jeanne	You, father dear, I knew that I should find,

And I once more should kiss your kind, kind eyes.

Rahire   Well, 'tis a vast surprise, and oh

We must not part again. Where do you go?

Blondel   To Bethlehem, a faithful woman there

Will care and feed these little sheep, and bear

The burden with a mother's smiling face;

For all are mothers in that happy place

Where He was once a Child.

Rahire   His soldiers true,

Crusaders all, are marching to renew

Their holy vow before the little shrine

Where Christ was born, and by this sign (*points to the Red Cross*)

We pay our homage too before the door

Of that poor stable, open evermore.

Blondel   As humble offering from all sinful men,

Who seek to see thy gates, Jerusalem.

Rahire   To Bethlehem then and, guided by the star;

We find the place where all our treasures are.

(Curtain.)

Scene IV

Bethlehem

Woman   Now that tired eyes have slept and weary feet

Have rested well—they shall be first to greet

The little Lord Who lies in darkness there.

You shall light now His bed and so prepare

His shrine, that when the great Crusaders come

Here, where all roads meet from Trèves, from Rome,

Paris or London, Aix or Acquitaine,

The wandering stranger finds his home again.

Here is a light, now let the candles flare,

Show to all travelers that the Child is here.

Come, take it so, see how the lantern bright

Bids all poor stragglers welcome here tonight.

(Children light candles, hold lantern.)

Hugh   I hear a sound of music in the air.

Guy   The tramp of armèd knights; see, they draw near.

Jeanne   I see their armor shining like the sun.

Rahire   Praise be to God, my brothers, every one.

Blondel   Our Lord the King, Godfrey and many a knight

              Toil the steep road to worship here tonight.

Woman   From Bethlehem to Jerusalem they ride,

              Crusaders all, who at this holy tide

              Pause for a moment here to bow the knee

              The little Lord, lies smiling in the hay.

              (Crusaders march up the room.)

Rahire   The herald, see, advances to proclaim

              The rank and title of each noble name.

              Emperors and princes, warriors and kings,

              Leaving all pride, forgetting earthly things,

              With bended knee, bowed head and humbled heart,

              Tender their homage, and, so blest, depart.

(The procession, led by the Herald, advances up the center of the room, and as the Herald proclaims the name, each character in turn stands in the center of stage.)

Herald   Peter the Hermit.

Peter the Hermit (*Advances to center of stage.*)

A hermit I, among the stony wastes,

Serving my God in silence alone,

Yet fared I forth to set the world ablaze,

Vassal in field, or Emperor on the throne.

I urged them all to danger and to death,

Counting the vain things of the world but dross,

And the vast army moved across the world

Under the standard of the blood-red cross.

To save the shrine from heathen hands, to speed

The pious pilgrim on the unknown way.

Much did they gain, much lose for that wild dream,

A dream that vanished with the waking day.

Herald (*In a loud voice proclaims*)

       Field Or, Lion Rampant Sable, Godfrey de Bouillon.

       (Godfrey de Bouillon, with page bearing crown on a cushion, advances and stands in center of stage.)

Godfrey   I, Godfrey of Boulogne, a crownèd king,

       Though never I that crown have worn.

       How should I bear the golden crown

       Where Christ wore crown of thorn?

       Jerusalem's king. I pray one prayer,

       To lie within her sacred walls,

       Feet crossed, eyes closed, and sword in hand,

       Till the last trumpet calls.

Herald   Field gules, Three Lions Passant Or,

       The King of England.

Richard

Coeur De Lion

> They call me Richard of the lion heart,
>
> Yet tenderer that heart than any lion,
>
> That so had loved my England's happy hills
>
> More than the hills of Zion.
>
> I, Lord of that fair belovèd land,
>
> Must ride the arid ways in desert bare,
>
> For that high purpose and the glorious gain
>
> That I might never share.
>
> Jerusalem, the holy city, fades
>
> Into a mist, and towers of London shine
>
> Through prison bars—alas! my lion heart,
>
> No heart so sad as mine.

Herald Field Argent, Chevron Gules, Three Mullets of the Field,

The Queen of England.

Berengaria

A Princess of Navarre and England's Queen,

With what secure, enchanted feet

I followed my great lord across the world

In winter's cold and summer's heat.

From Cyprus and the sound of wedding bells

To Acre's walls and Ascalon,

I watched and waited as the battle turned

For victory to Christendom.

And there was naught save blunder and defeat

And the great army rolled away,

And on Jerusalem's hills and mighty gates

A Christless people pray.

Herald   Cross Patè, Sable, Field Argent, The Knight Templar.

The Knight

Templar I am Gerald of Bideford,

Bideford in Devon,

Where soft airs blow and tiny larks

Sing in blue heaven.

A Templar Knight; my Cross

Black on my snow-white shield,

I dwelt in Nazareth's holy streets

That would not yield.

Yet when the heathen rode

Outside that city walled,

And uttered loud the words of shame,

Then honor called.

And on the Horns of Hattin

The blood of men flowed red

For the great cause lost, and on the sand

Our mighty dead.

Herald   Field Azure, Three Fleur de Lys Or, The King of France.

Philip of France

A true Crusader I,

Philip of France,

Master of horse and sword,

Bearer of lance.

Builder of Paris walls,

Strong walls and bare,

Hold fast a city great,

Paris the fair.

And if Jerusalem

Saladin gain,

Paris shall lift her crown

Over the Seine.

Her mighty towers shall rise

Crown of the world

When all swords are dust,

All banners furled.

This my royal will:

Let the bells ring

From the towers of Notre Dame,

Saith Philip the King.

Herald   Part-per-Pale, Dexter Field Azure, Seme of Fleur de Lys Or,

Sinister Field Argent Castle Gules,

Tancred of Tiberias.

Tancred   Lord of Tiberias, called great Tancred, I,

I fought as Christian Knight

When at the last I leapt the holy wall

And saw the sacred light.

What should I do as God's true soldier, then,

When brave men, mad with rage,

Slew without mercy those defenseless folk

Like wild birds in a cage.

I stayed the slaughter in the holy place,

Where Christ had stood to bless

The poor children dear, the outcast and the poor,

The weary and oppressed.

With Tancred then shall seal of mercy rest,

Who gave the kiss of peace

To heathen men, to friend and foe, and gained

His own soul's release.

(Each Crusader after his speech retires to back of stage and kneels before the lighted manger.)

THE CRUSADERS' CAROL

All Standing. Sing:

The Shepherds found Thee by night, by night,

Seeing the star so bright, so bright.

Ah me, it was a goodly sight

On Christmas Day in the morning.

Three Kings came from the East, the East,

The great to pray with the least, the least,

Ready to keep the Holy Feast

On Christmas Day in the morning.

The strangest sight they saw, they saw,

A Child on a bed of straw, of straw,

Their souls were filled with holy awe

On Christmas Day in the morning.

You that have come from afar, afar,

Soldier of His in war, in war,

Come, oh come, where the true hearts are

On Christmas Day in the morning.

Enter here by the door, the door,

Down on your knees on floor, on floor,

The Lord of all you come to adore

On Christmas Day in the morning.

This, Christian men, is your inn, your inn,

Brothers in arms one kin, one kin,

Your host a Babe born without sin

On Christmas Day in the morning.

Sing you good will to men, to men,

Glory to God in the Highest, and then,

Praise to the Babe in Bethlehem

On Christmas Day in the morning.

(Curtain)

EPILOGUE

We tried to paint a picture of another age,

With half-awakened eyes to turn the golden page

That told how even children wandered out afar,

Aflame with fire to conquer in that holy war;

How with their fathers brave they too lie in the dust,

Their little bows all broken, their little lances rust.

The nations watched them pass to danger and to death,

With tired eyes and disappointed hearts beneath

The blood-red cross. Who knows perhaps they did surmise,

That victory comes alone to innocent hands and eyes:

What sinful man could never see these children dear

Might see, Jerusalem's sacred hills, and without fear

Enter the holy place. And if the old men dreamed,

The young saw visions. Forgive us that it seemed

We too might share the dream. And if this play

Of childish ventures, childish hopes and fears, today

Gave these things instant life, then we are quite content

To have it so. Friends, the hours are well-nigh spent,

Night comes apace. Our happy task is ended now.

Before we part to all in gratitude we bow

That you in generous kindness read our story right

And so rewarded us. Sweet friends, good night, good night.

SIR CLEGES

DRAMATIS PERSONAE

Prologue

Sir Cleges

His Wife

Margaret \

Hugh   His children

Catherine /

King Arthur

Queen Guinevere

Lancelot

Sir Galahad

A Nun

Sir Tristram

Iseult

A Soldier

A Herald

Lord Chamberlain

Messenger

Pages, Ladies, and Knights of the Court, etc.

Epilogue

Notes: Music for Carols, "Cherry Tree Carol" (traditional) available free on line at http://www.8notes.com/scores/3892.asp and "How Far Is It To Bethlehem?" (Sheet music available http://www.sheetmusicplus.com/title/How-far-is-it-to-Bethlehem/4423230)

PROLOGUE

We here present to you in halting rhyme

From the grey twilight of an older time

A story. Time was when Arthur ruled our land

And gathered round his royal state a band

Of knights, vowed to a holy quest and noble deeds,

Treading the way of virtue where it leads

To peace and sweet content in far-off Avalon,

That lovely city of oblivion

Where spring eternal blooms. That each should hold

His soul more dear than fame, or land, or gold,

He bade them fight the grievous sin of pride

That subtly tempteth all men—and abide

In that fair heritage of all the meek,

The kingdom of God's poor—to help the weak

To stand upright, to comfort the oppressed,

And treat the hungry as an honored guest.

And this our little legend plainly shows

How pride was humbled, and, who knows,

We, children of another day, may find

In this old tale some pleasure for the mind.

And so we players offer of our best,

Your kind indulgence well may do the rest.

Scene I—*The interior of a poor cottage. Sir Cleges chopping wood. His wife busied with various things. She might be spinning or mending, or setting the room to rights. A fire of sticks, if possible.*

Cleges   Dear heart, you work too hard, indeed I say,

For me and for the children, every day

To wash, to spin, to bake and clean and mend,

You that once rode a horse, had gold to spend,

Jewels to wear, and were in truth a queen.

Wife   Ah, love, forget the things that once have been

For me, I mind them not, but yet for you,

If we could have our home again, renew

Our life among our own loved lands,

No matter then that these poor hands

Are scarred and rough, my beauty gone—

Cleges   Ah, love, be done, be done.

The fault is mine; I did not husband gifts

That God had given, but like one who drifts,

I let the tide of pleasure bear me on,

And houses, lands, and treasure, all are gone.

Wife   No, no, you trusted overmuch, and thought

That all men lived as guileless as they ought,

And when they gave in trust their plighted word

No thought of false deceit within you stirred.

You loved the poor—you gave them of your best—

Meat, drink, and clothing and a place of rest;

No beggar ever left our door unfed,

And every little child was comforted.

Cleges   Dear love, you are a spirit rare and brave,

Your lips are smiling, but your eyes are grave,

Life has been hard, but yet it's very sweet

Where woman is and sound of little feet.

Wife   I hope the children will be coming soon,

It's getting dark, tonight there is no moon.

Cleges   But it is Christmas Eve, and angels fair

Guard all young things tonight with heavenly care,

For love of Mary's Son, the little Child

Laid in a manger when the wind blew wild.

Wife   King Arthur summons 'specially tonight

The ladies of his court, and every knight

That holds a place within his Table Round,

And in past years Sir Cleges had been found

Amongst the noblest at the great king's feast.

Cleges   Who now has not a place among the least,

Who stands in rags, who cannot find a gift,

Who, seeing his lord his eyes he could not lift,

A beggar, poor and cold, a laughing-stock

At whom the very servants of the king make mock.

Wife   Oh, had we the smallest gift to give

The king on Christmas Day, I do believe

He'd welcome his true knight and once again

Justice be done.

Cleges   And we have none. (*Despairingly*)

(*Enter three children excitedly.*)

Margaret   Mother, Father, look, look what we have found,

Cherries—

Hugh   Growing upon that old tree round

By the dark pond. The tree that bears no fruit,

And Father said was dead right from the root.

Catherine   I saw the cherries first, and Hugh climbed up

And picked and picked until he had enough

For all of us, and Margaret said that we

Must bring them home for both of you to see.

Cleges   Cherries in December! Cherries in the snow.

What does it mean, children, how should I know?

God gave me gifts, and those are taken away,

Yet gives me cherries on a Christmas Day.

Hugh   I heard sweet singing near the old dead tree.

Margaret   I saw a wondrous light in front on me.

Catherine   I saw Our Lady's face, and oh she smiled,

And in her arms she held the Holy Child.

Wife   Praise be to God. Praise to His glorious Name

Who raised the dead, gave feet unto the lame,

Sight to the blind, and for us poor folk

A miracle has wrought.

(*To Cleges.*)   Come find your cloak,

Your staff, your sword, and hasten to the King,

When such a present in your hand you bring

He will accord a royal welcoming.

(*Wife and Children help Sir Cleges with cloak, etc.*)

Cleges   The mystery is too deep for us, my wife,

The barren bears—and dead things come to life,

St. Joseph too found cherries on a tree

In winter time, come sing that song for me.

CHERRY TREE CAROL

Joseph was an old man,

An old man was he,

He married sweet Mary

The Queen of Galilee.

As they went a-walking

In the garden so free,

Maid Mary spied cherries

Hanging on a tree.

Mary said to Joseph

With her sweet lips so mild,

"Pluck those cherries, Joseph,

For to give to my child."

Oh then replied Joseph

With words so unkind,

"I will pluck no cherries

To give to thy child."

Mary said to cherry tree,

"Bow down to my knee

That I may eat cherries

One, two and three."

The uppermost sprig then

Bowed down to her knee,

Thus you may see, Joseph,

These cherries are for me"

Oh, eat your cherries, Mary,

Oh eat your cherries now,

Oh, eat your cherries, Mary,

That grow upon the bough.

(For an idea of the melody, you may listen here: http://www.youtube.com/watch?v=C8n00BLTS5k -- Ed.)

(CURTAIN)

Scene II

The King's Procession to the Christmas Feast. The procession should march up the room to the stage, each character standing in front and, after speaking, passing out at back of stage.

Arthur   I am that great king of old who rode

With all his knights to Camelot,

Who shared their mirth, but bore the load

Of grief…By friend betrayed, by love forgot,

To whom the heavenly vision was denied

Though heart should ache and passion burn,

Who saw no Grail, whose spirit died

When hate and evil things abroad did ride,

But who shall come again when men discern

The hidden things of God. Then shall the king return.

Queen   And I unhappiest queen. Set on a throne,

Whom none might question or refuse

To reverence there. Whose treachery alone

Broke his great heart, so did I lose

My honor and his love—so did I shame

The glory of his Table Round,

And my unholy love like a spent flame

Flicked and flared and sank into the ground.

Lancelot   Men called me first and best of Arthur's knights,

First in the lists and first at foe.

Yet was my soul hid from him. Heights

Where he dwelt lonely, so that he might not know

How men may sin and suffer endless pain

For mortal love, and ever bear

Upon their golden shield the stain

Of honor broken and a fair faith slain.

Such am I who loved Queen Guinevere,

Loved to my hurt and hers, and loved in vain.

Tristram   Sir Tristram I, more venturous than they all,

Who rode the plains and crossed the sea—

Saw the great towers of Spain, the hills of France,

And to my doom set sail for Brittany.

Iseult   God gave me mighty power with these white hands

To heal those sick to death. Iseult

Of Ireland I—and yet I could not save

Sir Tristram, who I loved—the guilt

Is mine—who first betrayed his trust

So that he died in misery alone,

His fair fame gone, his honor in the dust.

Galahad   And I the youngest knight, great Lancelot's son,

Was but a boy—and like a boy

I fought and feasted, held that none

Could drink so deeply of the well of joy.

But now 'tis gone. I move as in a dream

Along the pathways of the earth,

Vision alone is real, and I seem

To see again through open heaven the beam

That showed that Cup of peerless worth,

So I enchanted ride, in glory all supreme.

Nun   And I that nun, sister to Percivale,

Who prayed and fasted, and did see

In the red morn the vision of the Grail,

Through parted clouds the heavenly mystery.

(Enter Sir Cleges.)

(In front of 1ˢᵗ Curtain.)

Soldier   Halt, your name, you cannot pass this way.

Cleges   Cleges my name, I seek the King today.

Soldier   You seek the King? A beggar and in holes

Your wretched cloak; there are no likely doles

For such as you. The King sits in his hall

And feasts with noble knights—and you of all

Would be the scorn did I admit you there.

You cannot pass; away, get out of here.

Cleges   I am a knight of Arthur's Table Round.

Soldier   Beggar and liar, look that you be not found

Anigh this door; stand back, away, be off.

Cleges   And yet I think you will not dare to scoff

            When what is hid beneath my rags you see—

(produces cherries)

            Ripe cherries grown upon a barren tree

            In winter time. And by Our Lady's grace

            Gift for the King.

Soldier   A miracle indeed, perhaps I ought

            To let him pass—a wonder that I had not thought

            Is here. The King most certainly will give

            A large reward for that, and as I live,

            I'll claim a third of it to let you through.

Cleges   It is agreed, a third of it.

(In front of 2ⁿᵈ curtain.)

Herald   Halt, your name, you cannot pass this way.

Cleges   Cleges my name, I seek the King today.

Herald   Know you not the King is feasting in his hall

With all the great. No wretched man shall crawl

Into his sight with sniveling tale and whine

Some lying story and by that incline

His ear to mercy. Get you gone, I say,

No beggar enters through these doors today.

Cleges   God grant me patience. True I am very poor,

But not without an offering do I seek the door

To my King's presence. It shall surely be

Open, and my gift accepted royally,

For never has man seen what here I bear—

Cherries of June, grown not when sun shines clear

But in the bitter cold of yesterday

Upon a thrice dead tree. And now I may

Pass to the King.

Herald   True, he holds there a mystery in his hand;

I'll let him through. But you must understand

That if the King should give you a reward

One third is mine—never to be restored.

Cleges　　One third of the King's gift is to be yours, I

understand.

(In front of third curtain.)

Chamberlain　Halt, your name. You cannot pass this way.

Cleges　　Cleges my name, I seek the King today.

Chamberlain　Cleges, I know you, for you once were seen

At my lord's table, now so poor and lean

I thought you a mere beggar such as begs

For crusts and broken bits and wine cup dregs

There in the gutter. Once you wore armor fine,

Cloak like to this, a tunic just like mine,

Now stand ashamed, a matter for a jest,

Who come on Christmas Day in all your best

Attire to see your King. You scarecrow, hence,

Out of my sight. Back to the hovel whence you came.

Cleges   My lord, I know you too. It's very sure

I'm poor and hungry so that I must endure

Your insults. Yet do I bring a treasure

Unto my King and so would do him pleasure.

Chamberlain Treasure, what treasure could you bring the King?

You that lost all and have not anything?

Cleges   Yet so it is. Some blessed saint has wrought

A miracle—I in my rags have brought

This gift unto the King. Cherries from heaven

Grown in the dark and cold of winter even

Upon an old dead tree.

Chamberlain In truth a marvel! It will delight the King.

He'll give a great reward for any holy thing.

Come, Cleges, come, I'll send thee to my lord,

But ere I let you pass, your plighted word,

To give to me one-third of that reward

The King gives you—one-third, one-third, one-third.

Cleges A third is yours, I heard, I heard, I heard.

(Curtain.)

Scene III—The King's Court

King Friends, we have feasted, as indeed is right

Upon His birthday Who was born this night,

But ere our revels and our dance begin

Sing we the birth song of the new-born King.

CAROL

How Far Is It To Bethlehem?

How far is it to Bethlehem?

    Not very far.

Shall we find the stable room

    Lit by the Star?

Can we see the little Child,

    Is He within?

If we lift the wooden latch

    May we go in?

May we stroke the creatures there,

    Ox, ass and sheep?

May we peep like them and see

    Jesus asleep?

If we touch His tiny hand

    Will he awake?

Will He know we've come so far

    Just for His sake?

Great Kings have precious gifts

And we have nought;

Little smiles and little tears

Are all we brought.

For all weary children

Mary must weep,

Here on His bed of straw

Sleep, children, sleep.

God in His Mother's arms,

Babes in the byre,

Sleep, as they sleep who find

Their Heart's Desire.

(As the Carol ends, Sir Cleges enters at the door and a Messenger steps forward.)

Messenger   Your name and purpose here?

Cleges   My name is Cleges, and I seek my King,

Nor come I empty-handed, for I bring

Such wonder here concealed, such treasure rare

That all will stand amazed and 'wildered stare.

Messenger   I will announce your business to my lord.

(Goes to the King and whispers in his ear.)

King   Bid him approach. Sir Cleges at my board

Was faithful knight and true. But I had lost

His company, so that I sorrowed most

When in the fight I missed him from the tale

Of these my knights who sought the Holy Grail.

Cleges   My liege—I who was rich am poor and sad,

I dwell apart and forfeit all I had,

Yet servant of my King and knight born free,

Grant me my boon. Receive my gift from me.

(Kneeling—Gives cherries.)

Queen   What miracle is this, do cherries grow

When winter rules and earth is wrapped in snow?

Has Merlin worked enchantments for my lord

That winter turns to summer at a word?

Cleges   No Merlin, lady, but the Queen of Heaven

Perchance had touched the tree and given

Blossom and fruit that once was dead and done

As she gave life unto God's Blessed Son.

Galahad   Mysteries are around us everywhere,

And God works mighty things for those that He

Holds dear.

King   In all true humbleness I take the gift

Come from on high, and ask you all to lift

Your voices now in joyfulness and praise

To Him Whose power is shown in wonderous ways.

TE DEUM LAUDAMUS

(About six verses in Latin to a chant.)

King   Now that our thanks and praise are rendered

     It is but meet that a reward be tendered

     To good Sir Cleges whom the saints have blessed.

     Your lands I do restore. But for the rest

     Choose what reward you will, for it is yours.

Cleges   My wife and children wait without the doors,

     But ere I tell my joyful news I pray

     One boon. My lord, take this my stick and lay

     Nine strokes upon my back, but let the blows

     Fall lightly, though well my good arm knows

     Where they shall next fall heavily, and then,

     True justice being done, the odds are even.

King   A strange request! Granted for my word's sake,

     Lightly they fall, Sir Cleges need not quake

Though beaten by a King.

(Cleges kneels and the King strikes him nine times, lightly.)

Cleges *(Rushing at the Guard)* A third of my reward as you would ask.

It's yours—it's yours—it's yours, *(Strikes him three times.)*

a glorious task.

Thus to fulfill a promise truly made,

Accounts are squared and all my debt is paid.

(Rushes at the King's Herald.)

Cleges And here's a third for you, you knave,

Pride has a fall, here's the reward you crave—

One, two, and three, *(Strikes him three times.)*

it serves you very right

Who had insulted one who was Arthur's knight.

(Rushes at the Lord Chamberlain.)

Cleges And here's the last…

Take your reward, well may you stand aghast

To find your punishment, you rat, you rat, you rat

Now then, stand still, take that and that and that.

(Strikes him three times.)

(Turns to the King.)

Cleges　　My lord, they treated me with pride and scorn,

Laughed at my rags, my misery forlorn,

Forbade me entrance to my King until

I showed the wonder cherries. They did but fill

Their hearts with greed, they asked a third

Of what reward the King might give. You heard

How I have kept my word.

King　　Contempt and pride are of the fiends of hell,

Therefore, Sir Cleges, you have done right well

To lay them in the dust. Yet know we may

Be often sore beset along the narrow way

Of truth and humbleness which ends

In a poor stable, where a Mother bends

Low o'er the cradle of her sleeping Child,

The power of God, His glory undefiled.

ADESTE FIDELES

(To be sung kneeling.)

Adeste fideles,

Laeti triumphantes;

Venite, venite in Bethlehem;

Natum videte,

Regem Angelorum:

Refrain:
Venite adoremus,

Venite adoremus,

Venite adoremus Dominum!

En grege relicto humiles ad cunas

Vocati pastores ad properant;

Nosque ovanti gradu festinemus.

Refrain

Aeterni Parentis splendorem aeternum

Velatum sub carne videbimus;

Deum infantem pannis involutum.

Refrain

Pro nobis egenum et foeno cubantem

Piis fovemus amplexibus!

Sic nos amantem quis non redamaret.

Refrain

Deum de Deo,

Lumen de lumine

Gestant puellae viscera,

Deum verum, Genitum non factum

Refrain

(*Curtain.*)

EPILOGUE

To all assembled here our thanks are due

Who've listened to our little play—for you

Must know we greatly feared that this old tale

Might prove too simple, and that we should fail

To hold your thoughts. But because greed and pride

Still walk abroad and in high places ride,

Take you the staff of good Sir Cleges there

And put the mighty down—lest unaware

Stand starving at your doors the brave and true,

And beggarmen be better men than you;

And charities, when woods are bare and grey

Be rare as cherries on a Christmas Day.

THE CHILDREN'S CRUSADE
SIR CLEGES
THE CHRISTMAS GIFT

THREE PLAYS FOR CHILDREN

By

FRANCES CHESTERTON

Price Two Shillings net

THE CHRISTMAS GIFT

Dramatis Personae

The Grandmother

The Mother

The Father

Marie

Pierre

Jeanne

A Playing Boy

Two Other Boys

A Poor Woman

You can compose your own melody for the songs included in this play.

This little play is meant for very young children, and can of course be lengthened by additional carols. One of the singing boys should, if possible, accompany the carol on a flageolet (recorder) or pipe.

Scene—*Interior of a peasant's hut, furnished in Flemish fashion. At the back, but conspicuous, a Christmas Manger. Table with check cloth spread for a simple meal (coffee-pot, bread, cheese, apples).*

Mother and children seated.

Grandmother in her arm-chair at the back, by stove or fire.

Pierre (*to Marie*)   Can I have one more tiny bit of bread?

I am still hungry.

Marie   You know what Mother said.

A little must be left lest some poor soul,

Homeless and starving, should request a dole,

And it is Christmas Eve.

Mother   Yes, it is Christmas Eve, and we must not forget

To smile. A brave boy will not fret

While Father fights afar for this dear land

And all of us.

For we know where'er he wanders

His heart is still at home with us in Flanders.

And Pierre, when you are big, you too shall fight

With all the holy saints to guard the right.

Come, Marie, clear the plates and cups away,

Pierre, move the chairs, and little Jeanne shall take

Dear Grannie's hand, and everyone must make

Haste to have all in order.

Grandmother   Ah, dear me,

(Turning to the children.)

Poor little souls, tonight you cannot kneel

In our dear church, I am old and tired. I feel

That I shall die, nothing but ruin and the awful fire

That burns and burns.

Jeanne   Grannie, don't cry, because I love you so.

(Kisses her.)

Mother   Now children, stand there quietly in a row.

Pierre, light the candles at the little shrine.

(He does so.)

Mother   There, that is right. Come, children mine,

We won't forget to keep the holy night.

Though all is dark, here is the little light.

(Holds up a candle.)

Mother   To welcome him, the helpless newborn child,

To our poor home.

(There is a knock at the door.)

Grannie   Ah, who is that, is it a cruel foe?

Mother   No, Grannie, no. Come in, my boys, from out the snow.

(Opens door.)

1st Boy   We saw a light and so we ventured near.

2nd Boy   We're singing boys, and that's why we are here.

There is no choir to sing in, all is gone.

The altars, shrines, one mass of broken stone.

Marie   Indeed, we know. But see our tiny Manger.

Pierre   Our little Lord must never be a stranger.

Jeanne   And here He is, and now we all can sing.

Mother   Come, boys, this is a Christmas welcoming.

(The children kneel or stand on each side of the Manger.)

CAROL

Welcome, welcome, little Lord,

Out of the cold dark night.

We want to give Thee all we have

Of love and warmth and light.

We have no gold, incense or myrrh

To lay at Thy dear feet,

Only our little lips and hands

That offer service meet.

Our little songs to sing Thee now

Just softly to Thy sleep,

Our little prayers to comfort Thee

When Thou for us must weep.

Come, share with us our little feast,

Be with us at our board

On this, the happiest night of nights,

Oh welcome, little Lord.

*(The carol "Welcome, welcome" works to the tune known as the "Tallis Canon,"
used for "O Holy Spirit Come To Us", except that one must add in an initial
"O" —so the first line will have eight syllables, like this: O welcome, welcome little
Lord. Also, the Tallis hymn is can be sung as a canon—a round—like "Row,
row, row your boat"—Ed.)*

Mother   You must have food and drink before you start.

(Marie and Jeanne get it ready.)

1ˢᵗ Boy   We thank you, Madam, from our very heart.

2ⁿᵈ Boy   We visit many other homes this Christmas Eve

                  To cheer the folks and bid them all believe

                  The miserable time will pass away.

                  And give them hope to face the Christmas Day.

3ʳᵈ Boy   And so with warmest thanks we say farewell,

                  Peace to this house and all who therein dwell.

(They go out.)

Grandmother These boys indeed have given me strength again,

To face the peril and the bitter pain.

Jeanne If Father were but here, I feel I'd like to dance.

Mother Dance, little one, dance, while you have the chance.

(She dances a few steps.)

(A knock at the door.)

Pierre Another knock, who can it be?

Marie I'll see. I'll see.

Beggar Woman (*enters*)

Have pity on me, I am well nigh dead.

The snow is deep. I have no food or bed.

The soldiers drove me out; let me get warm.

I'll soon be off. I won't do any harm.

Mother   Come in, good friend, there's not much here to

spare,

But what there is you're welcome to a share.

Pierre   Here's milk.

Marie   Here's bread.

Jeanne   And here's a bit of cheese.

Grannie   Come near the stove, I'm sure that you will freeze

There by the door.

Woman (*suddenly sees the Manger.*)

'Tis the holy night.

And here the little crib, ah, heavenly sight.

(*She kneels a moment.*)

Woman   I thought He had no place, no home, no bed,

This land a desert, no stone to lay His head.

Yet here He lies in smiling sweet content,

A refuge found for Him our God has sent.

Grannie   A refuge too, for you, if you will have it so.

Marie   Yes, stay with us, we will not let you go.

Mother   Grannie just needs a friend with whom to chat

Whilst I am busy over this and that.

Woman   I thank you from my heart, dear friend.

Gladly I'll stay until this terror ends.

(She seats herself opposite the Grandmother, near the stove, sipping and eating slowly.)

Mother   And now it's time you children went to sleep.

It's very late, and see the shadows creep

Upon the wall. Marie, undo Jeanne's frock,

Pierre, bolt the door, for no one else will knock.

(A knock.)

Marie   Who can it be?

Jeanne   Mother, I feel afraid.

Pierre   It is a soldier.

Grandmother   Alas! we are betrayed.

(Another knock.)

Mother   Who's there?

(Opens the door a little.)

Voice (*Outside*)   Don't you know me, don't you see?

Father (*enters*)   Wife, Mother, children, who else could it be?

Mother   Henri! My husband!

Children (*all*)   Father, Father dear.

Grannie   My son, my son.

(*Embraces.*)

Father (*To Beggar Woman.*)   And who is this?

Mother   Our friend, who else had none.

Father   Then doubly welcome. It is Christmastide.

Who asks for shelter then can never be denied.

Marie   Father, what's that you've got beneath your cloak?

Father   A gift to please the eyes of little folk.

              A gift I found upon the battlefield.

Mother   And all this time you've kept the gift concealed.

Father   This gift, dear heart, you'll see I could not leave

              Orphaned, deserted on a Christmas Eve.

              Mother, sit here; come children, look and see,

              I lay my Christmas gift on Mother's knee.

(Undoes his cloak and places a newborn child on Mother's lap.)

Marie   A baby, and for us; oh, Father dear.

Pierre   I'll fight for it when I'm a man, no fear.

Father   Did I do well, my wife, did I do well?

(She nods.)

Jeanne *(Awestruck)*   Is it the Baby Jesus?

Mother   Oh children, who can tell?

(Curtain.)

Acting Edition, 1102.

PIERS PLOWMAN'S PILGRIMAGE

A Morality Play

BY

FRANCES CHESTERTON
(MRS. G. K. CHESTERTON)

MUSIC ARRANGED AND COMPOSED BY

BRIDGET MULLER

LONDON:
SAMUEL FRENCH, LTD.
26 SOUTHAMPTON ST.
STRAND, W.C.2

NEW YORK:
SAMUEL FRENCH
25 WEST 45th STREET

ONE SHILLING AND SIXPENCE NET

PIERS PLOWMAN'S PILGRIMAGE

A Morality Play

(From Will Langland's great Epic of a May Morning on the Malvern Hills)

By

Frances Chesterton (Mrs. G.K. Chesterton)

Music Arranged and Composed by Bridget Muller

Original copyright, 1925

CHARACTERS

Piers Plowman

Conscience

Luxury

Gluttony

Sloth

Pride

Wrath

Envy

Avarice

Repentance

Hope

Poor Woman

Humility

Purity

Contentment

Temperance

Courage

Peace

Charity

Deeds

Do Well

Innocence

The Enemy

Will Langland

and

Various Characters in Field of Folk

The original music for this play was sold separately and has, to date, not been found. —Ed.

ARGUMENT

Prologue—Will Langland speaks.

Scene 1—A Field of Folk. Piers Plowman passes. Conscience sets him on his Pilgrimage.

Scene 2—A High Road. Piers meets his Enemy and is sore beset by Vices, but is saved by Repentance and led by Hope to———

Scene 3—The Door of the House of Truth, before which the Seven Virtues stand sentinel.

Scene 4—Piers is turned from the door by Deeds and goes forth to labor with his hands, to share his all with Poverty, and to forgive his Enemy.

Scene 5—Purged of all evil, Piers returns at last to Truth's fair House and enters on his Heritage, the great Reward which nobly, beyond Death, proclaims the end.

Epilogue—Langland commends his Vision to the Future.

Prologue

(A short overture before the prologue. A dance in 2/4 time for the rise of the Curtain.)

Will Langland:

Here stand I, Will Langland, that poor poet

Who, ah me, how long ago on Malvern hills

Saw that fair vision of a field of folk

While o'er me sang the birds, and at my feet

The little brook murmured unceasingly.

There lay the world and all the men thereof,

Monarchs and jesters, emperors and knights,

Strong men and babes, merchants and holy priests,

Poor men and rich, oppressors and oppressed,

And journeying among them Ploughman Piers

Ever questioning, ever seeking truth.

And now these children of another day

Would have you see as through the centuries dim

That ploughman as of old still wandering wide,

And for a moment in a childish guise

They tell the ancient story once again

'Tis very simple, but I crave your leave

These children to commend. I love them well

Who have loved me enough to act this tale

Of my poor ploughman and his endless search

Through the long aeons of that pilgrimage

That ends alone when man himself shall end.

SCENE 1

Scene—*A field full of folk, a seller, two countrywomen, a quack doctor, a minstrel, a jester, a nobleman, a peasant, a little cripple, a pieman, a dancer, a fine lady,* Conscience, *and* Piers.

A Seller   (*at a booth*) Come, Mistress, what will you buy? Eggs, butter, cheese, linen, laces, ribbons, trinkets; all are here!

First Woman   Butter and cheese I can make better than any you can sell; and give true weight I do, no cheating from me; but ribbons and laces, that's another story; well, let's look!
    (*A little bargaining goes on.*)

Second Woman	Have you a remedy for an aching tooth, good sir?
Seller	Aye, that I have.
Doctor (*pushing by*)	Nay, believe him not, but I have a cure that will relieve all ills. Pain in the head, pain in the leg, pain in the arms, boils, fevers, agues, even the plague itself!
Second Woman	Ah! Let me have it!
Doctor	But it costs dear.
Second Woman	No matter for that. I can bear this pain no longer— (*hands over some money*)—it is a heavy price.
Doctor (*aside*)	Ah, that was well done, a little bread, some bitter aloe, and she thinks she has a cure for every ache and pain. Truly, it is easy to gain money this way.
Piers	Ah me, there goes a wicked man, and a silly woman.
Minstrel	Come good folk, come listen to my song.
Crowd	A song, a song, give us a song.
Minstrel (*song*)	"Come young men and young maids,
	Love time is here,
	What pleasure, what treasure

At the spring of the year.

Come sad folk, come dull folk

Leave trouble awhile———"

Jester (*pushes him aside*)

Enough, enough, have you no wits, he wants your pence; I only want your goodwill!

Piers

A good song is worth paying for, friend, and methinks goodwill is only bought with pence, too.

Jester

Aye, indeed it is, young master, what give you for mine?

Piers

Nothing at all, I know you, you are a false knave.   (*Hustles him off.*)

(*Enter a* Noble.)

Peasant

God keep thee my good lord, a boon!

Noble

Boon, what boon?

Peasant

I cannot plead my cause in the courts, no judge, no lawyer will listen to a poor man. My lord, uphold my cause, robbers have taken my land; my very life whereby I live!

Noble

Ah, I have heard that lying tale before, begone, take yourself off I say! (*Hits the poor man.*)

Piers	Noble and lord he is now, and yet tomorrow nothing, he has forgotten the law to be just, show mercy, and hear the poor man's cause. Alas! that rich men should so handle the poor.

(A little Cripple *enters bearing a candle.)*

Piers	Where go you, little friend?
Child	To church to give my candle to St. Francis.
Piers	To St. Francis?
Child	Yes, because he is as poor as I. I have no one to care for me except St. Francis.
Piers	Are you hungry, child?
Child	I am indeed, and I have far to go.
Pieman	Pies hot, all hot, good pies, best pies, come, come and eat.
Piers (*to the child*)	And so you shall, come give this poor child a good meal, friend.
Pieman	And will he pay for it?
Piers	Alas, he cannot.
Pieman	Then he must go hungry.
Piers	That he shall not.

(Buys a pie for the child, who eats it slowly.)

Child	When I have a penny I will buy a candle for you

some day, stranger, and burn it before St. Francis.

Piers   Aye, do so.

(*Child goes off.*)

Piers   How can men allow a little child to starve? I feel sick unto death!

A Dancer   A round, a round, come all good folk, come and see me! A Spanish dance, a Flemish dance, a French dance, what ever you want. Come, Piers, dance with me!

Piers   Nay, I am too sad to dance.

Dancer   I am sad too, but what can I do but dance? 'Tis the only way to make a living.

Piers   'Tis a poor living that depends on a dance. Friend, what will you do when you are old, and can dance no more?

Dancer   Faith, I know not, die most likely, so that's why I dance now. Come, come, do not grudge it, a penny for a dance.

(*He dances a gavotte, collects money from the crowd, and passes off.*)

(*Enter a* Fine Lady)—(*as they pass*)—Good morning, Madam!

Piers   Good morning, Madam!

Lady   Good morning, Piers, what are you doing here in this vulgar crowd?

Piers   I search for an honest man.

Lady	And have you found such a one?
Piers	Nay, Madam, except for a little crippled boy.
Lady	Piers, you should leave these folks alone, they are silly souls who would sell themselves for a bit of bread or a drink of sour wine; not worth thinking about. But listen, Piers, I can show you things worthy of a man. What do you say to movies, concerts, the glories of the world! Come with me, Piers!
Piers	No, no, I have another road to go.
Lady	What road?
Piers	The truth is, I don't know, but I know 'tis a hard road and it will not let me go with you.
Lady	Well then, farewell, Piers, you must go your own way.
Piers	'Tis not my way, but go I must.

(Enter Conscience. Soft music from Gerontius to end of Scene 1)

Conscience	Piers...
Piers	Ah, who are you?
Conscience	Do you not know me, Piers, I am Conscience. I think once you knew me well, but lately you have forgotten me. What are you doing here, in this maze and medley?
Piers	Conscience, I cannot say, what does it all mean?

Conscience	When all pleasures are tried, when all things are done, there remains one treasure that all good men must seek. Truth is that treasure and truth alone can show you how to bear the evils of the world. Truth can set you free of the despair and troubles that fret your soul. 'Tis as a humble pilgrim, Piers, you must set out on the journey to find her where she dwells. The way is long and tedious, but the reward is sure. Will you go forth, Piers?
Piers	Good Conscience, I am so unhappy there is no other thing for me to do.
Conscience	Then take the pilgrim's staff, and a good journey to you, Piers.
Piers	I start indeed, but with how heavy a heart. Farewell, Conscience.
Conscience	Farewell, Pilgrim. (*Points the road he is to take.*)

Scene 2

Scene—*On a high road.* Piers—Enemy

Enemy	I hate you, coward and liar that you are!

Piers	You call me a coward, liar, you who betrayed my trust and called me friend?
Enemy	Trust! What trust I ask you?
Piers	Did I not trust you, did I not call you friend, and have you not dragged my name of honor in the dust, bereft me of my love, my very life? Traitor and coward, I say!
Enemy	I did but as I minded to, you did not guard your honor or your love.
Piers	You stole them from me though I trusted you as God Himself!
Enemy	You are too simple, Piers, for this world's ways, what do I care?! So here I leave you and go. Here's my last word to you! (*Hits him a blow and rushes off.*) Farewell! Fool Piers!
Piers	He is a traitor and a liar, yet how I loved him once! Never can I forgive him; he has robbed me of all I had. Now has come upon me the heaviest of all blows: To lose a friend, my dearest friend. I can bear no more. Alas! alas, most unhappy man that I am, evil is around me everywhere, and I can find no peace. The rich men have cruelly used the poor men, the poor men hate the rich, children are starved, priests have forgotten their holy vows, men lie and steal, feast for pleasure, or fast because they have no food; disease and death are on every hand, and I, where shall I go that I may find peace? I am driven forth from the places of

men to search for that which I can never find. Where does Truth dwell, and where is the place of her habitation? Yet, I would take my staff in my hand and strap my pack on my back, and set out on my quest for I can no longer abide in this terrible place.

(*Enter* Luxury)

Luxury Why, Piers, what are you doing here?

Piers I am setting forth on a journey for I wish to seek to find Truth.

Luxury Why, now, Piers, that cannot be. You cannot leave me behind to whom you have been beholden all your life. In what soft bed will you sleep? What fine clothes will you wear? What will you eat and drink on that journey? Piers, you have always loved me….stay with me, with Luxury who has served you so faithfully and well.

Piers (*wavering*) Alas! What can I do? Luxury, it is true that I love thee well and yet—Ah! who is this?

(*Enter* Gluttony)

Gluttony Ah, Piers, where are you going?

Piers A journey to find Truth.

Gluttony (*surprised*) A journey! And what food and drink will you take on that journey?

Piers	A loaf of bread, a skin of water.
Gluttony (*laughing*)	Well now, that is a good joke. Come, come, whoever heard of something like this? Bread and water. Why, stay here with me and see what food and drink your old friend Gluttony can provide! See here, pies, choice meats, fruits, sweets, jellies and rarest wines! Now for a feast! Come Piers, eat and drink with me, and I think we shall hear a little more about that journey!
Piers	You tempt me sorely. Perhaps one meal together before I start, for start I must.

(*Begins to eat.*)

Gluttony	Here comes another friend! Ah, welcome, brother Sloth!
Sloth	Ah, Piers, where are you going, so prepared it seems for travel?
Piers	I take the road in search of Truth.
Sloth	I would go with you but my limbs are tired and I would rather sleep. See, Piers, rest here with me awhile; no man can travel unless he sleeps first. Here, stretch out your legs and lay your head upon this soft pillow.
Piers	Ah, me, I long for sleep, but I must fare forth.

(Piers *lies on the ground*, Luxury, Gluttony, Sloth *surround him humming softly.*)

Piers   Ah me, I am undone! I cannot rise! Luxury,
                       Gluttony, Sloth, let me go, I must find Truth.
   (*They hold him down.*)
                       Ah, let me go free! (*Despairingly*) What shall I
                       do? I have served you all my life and now you
                       will not let me go. I hate you now, I grieve I
                       ever knew you. Ah me, what can I do? Who is
                       there to aid and deliver me from these friends? I
                       call for help, but who shall answer?
   (*Enter* Repentance.)

Repentance   Piers!

Piers   (*looking up*)   Ah, who is this so sad and woe begone?

Repentance   I am Repentance, and it is I alone can free you
                       from these men who have you in their thrall.
                       Look on them boldly, Piers, and look on me.
                       Which do you love the best?

Piers   I think I love your sad face more than all the
                       world.

Repentance   Then I can bid them go and leave you free.
   (*Turns to the three,* Luxury, Gluttony, Sloth)

                       Unloose your hands, begone! Your work with
                       Piers is done, leave him to me.

   (*They leave the stage.*)

Piers (*weeping bitterly*)   Repentance, hold me fast, I cannot stand
                       alone!

Repentance   I am your best friend, Piers! Those false friends,

Luxury, Gluttony, Sloth, have left you, but there are others who will meet you on the road you want to travel; but fear not, I will be with you to the world's far end. Call on me, I shall come.

(*Exit* Repentance.)

Piers   Heaven grant it may be so. (*Picks up the backpack and staff.*) Now fare I forth again to look for Truth. Here comes some swaggering folk. Who might they be?

(*Enter* Pride *and* Wrath.)

Pride   Ho! Piers, where are you going? You were looking so intently you never noticed me!

Piers   Ah! This is Pride! Pride, you and I can be friends no more!

Pride   Friends no more? Indeed, we are friends. Come, walk with me. (*Puts his arm around* Piers.) I have nothing to do with common folk that pass my way, for at least I am something better. No man has my looks, my learning, my wealth, my manners. Not the king himself can equal me in state and presence. I choose you for my friend. 'Tis a great thing to be a friend of Pride.

Piers   No, no, I can't go with you!

Wrath   Then come with me. I am Wrath, stronger than Pride. I send forth my voice and frighten men. I can lay them in the dust. Thunder and lightning are at my command. I can destroy and I can kill.

Piers   No, no, you terrify me, I can't go with you!

(Pride *and* Wrath *seize him.*)

Pride and **Wrath**   We have you Piers, we will not let you go!

Piers   Ah, woe is me, what shall I do?

(*Enter* Envy.)

Envy   Ah, I see that Pride and Wrath have you in their hands, and here come I, Envy, to hold you, too! How you have called upon me in the past, wanted my gold, my house, my strength, or my good looks. And I can give them to you now. But you must stay with us, give up the search for Truth, for Truth is a hard mistress to serve, but we will serve you well.

Piers   Envy, I know you, and you tempt me sorely. I would love to have all your gifts, poor wretched man that I am.

(*Enter* Avarice.)

Avarice   See, Piers, this will keep you here! (*Produces a bag of gold.*) This is to have the world at your command. With this you can be master, with the power of emperor or Pope, houses and lands, pomp and pleasure are to be bought with gold. Honor, and fame, and the goodwill of men, and all for gold, gold, gold.

Piers		Avarice, truthfully, you don't know how easily I would stay. But alas, I can't. No! No! No!
All Four Vices		No Piers, we hold you, we have you, you cannot go!
Piers	*(struggling)*	Oh help! Help! Help! Repentance help me, for I'm being tormented!

(*Enter* Repentance)

Repentance	No man ever called on me in vain. Piers, you should have nothing to do with these conceited guides: with Pride and Wrath, Avarice and Envy.
Piers	Free me from them, or else I will despair indeed!
Repentance	Those tears may save you yet. Just come to me and look at my face once more. Kneel at my feet and see the unholy shades that fade away. See, they have left poor Piers and here he stands, a-tremble and afraid, but clean of soul and ready to start on his holy pilgrimage.
Piers	I am fearful I may never gain my goal or see Truth upon her throne.
Repentance	Courage, poor Piers, see here where Hope comes with sweet words of comfort and cheer!

(*Enter* Hope)

Hope	*(singing)*	Hard is the way that thou must walk,

Pilgrim Piers.

Ever at thy heels doth pale Death stalk

But have no fears.

Hope is thy guide and friend,

With thee the way to wend

Unto the world's far end,

Pilgrim Piers.

Yours the brave soldier's part to play,

Pilgrim Piers.

To march ahead and never stay

For any fears.

The heavenly blow is bent

In the great firmament,

A sign to thee is sent,

Pilgrim Piers.

Take courage then, oh, lonely heart,

Pilgrim Piers.

Heed not the toil or cruel smart

And bitter jeers.

Follow my light afar, breaking thy prison bar,

On the furthest star,

Pilgrim Piers.

SCENE 3

Scene—*Soft music. Locked door of the House of Truth, guarded by the virtues* Humility, Contentment, Purity, Temperance, Courage, Peace *and* Charity.

(Enter Piers *and* Hope*)*

Hope   Hail, Pilgrim Piers, for thou hast set thy feet

Upon the narrow way to where Truth dwells

In all her beauty, absolute and free,

A sight for men distraught, bewildered here

You hold the single eye, and single heart

Unmoved by all the vain world's pomp and show

Remote from anger, lust and villainy,

Envy and treachery and false words of men

To seek her face and her fair face alone?

Piers   That would I do. So may I enter now?

(Advances to locked door.)

Hope   No, Piers, thy course is not yet run, for know

To whom a light is given is much more required

Than those who walk in darkness. Pilgrim Piers,

Thou hast fought well. These were thy friends,

Strong helpers of all striving, doubting men

When in thy desperate need Repentance kind

Drove off the shameful sins that strove to win

Thy soul from this dark road that thou must walk.

These are the friends of every Christian soul

Wayfaring here mid sorrow, shame, and sin.

Come, speak to Pilgrim Piers and give good words

Of counsel and of cheer.

(End soft music.)

Humility (*Song—these poems can be equally well recited instead of sung.*)

> Piers, I would have thee go thy road
>
> Clothed with holy fear.
>
> Who humble lives is fit to die
>
> When dread Death cometh near.
>
> For know this well, who holds by me
>
> Can Satan's self defy
>
> This little rod shall speed the soul
>
> That God shall lift on high.

Contentment (*Sung or said, as above.*)

> Happy the man, happiest of mortals he
>
> Whose quiet mind from vain desires is free.
>
> Whom neither hopes deceive nor fears torment
>
> But lives at peace and with himself content.
>
> For I, Contentment, bear the branch of joy,
>
> No chance can me disturb, no ill destroy.

Purity   (*Sung or said*) Ever hast thou desired me, Piers,

> The pure heart and the strong,
>
> That through the cloud the bright sun sees

The cleansing wind in the high trees

And hears the lark's song.

White is the flower, white the shield,

O wayfaring man,

For Purity shall be thy guide,

Body and soul as thou dost ride,

This world's brief span.

Temperance (*Sung or said*) The giver of all good gifts

That no man may abuse

In wisdom and in reason clear

To Judge, to rule, a course to steer

'Twixt much or less to choose.

Give thanks for all good gifts

That are so freely given

To love, to reverence and control,

To find thereby oh, pilgrim soul,

The narrow road to heaven.

Courage (*sung or said*) As the great saints have fought,

So fight thou;

The sword in thy hand,

The crown on thy brow.

Courage to nerve thy arm

For the right,

Ready to meet the foe

Clothed in might.

Courage that bore the saints

On the dark road

Till splendid death should come

To ease the load.

Courage that never fails,

O Pilgrim here,

Until the journey's end

Be of good cheer.

Peace (*sung or said*)   Carry me in thy heart and fear no ill,

Deeper than deepest sea when all is still,

Higher than highest mount to heaven's door,

Peace dwelleth with thee, Piers, for evermore.

No wrath can thee disturb, no noise dismay,

Nor the cold moon by night nor sun by day.

Hid deep within thy heart unmovèd peace

Till the end come and all wanderings cease.

Charity (*sung or said*)   I am the heart of burning love,

And like a fire

I mount and rise on holy wings

Higher and higher.

I am the mighty flame that burns

As love evermore,

To save and heal and to redeem

The outcast and poor.

All things of earth shall pass away,

Charity never.

The flaming lamp of fire divine

Burneth forever.

Hope Now thou art armed indeed and in good mind

To see fair Truth. Yet all is not yet done,

For, mark me well, the pilgrim soul must strive

By deeds to prove that he love Truth alone.

And first the Christian rule he must fulfill

That for himself and for his fellow man

He will observe the just and honest law

That keeps the turmoil of the rude world fixed

And free. And beyond that the nobler law

Of mercy rare that origin divine

That argues man the very child of God.

And last, oh Piers, knowing the mystic law

By which forgiveness heals the sorest wound,

Piers, are thou thus prepared to act?

Piers	I am ready. What wouldst thou have me do?

(*Enter* Deeds)

Hope	See here is Deeds, who will declare the road
	That thou must follow now. Good day, good Deeds!
Deeds	A greeting, Hope! A greeting, Pilgrim Piers!
Piers	Ere I see Truth I come to you, good Deeds,
	To know what I should do to gain my end.
Deeds	Why, Piers, the first is but a simple thing.
	Just this, no more. To labor with thy hands
	Faithfully and well, to earn an honest wage
	For work well done, thine acre truly ploughed.
	A good day's work demands a day's good pay.
	This is to *do Well*.
Piers	That can I do, and after that?
Deeds	That is a harder task, Friend Piers. For see,
	What thou hast truly earned, thou must not keep
	While poor men starve, and beggars go in rags,
	And mothers weep, and little children die,
	But thou must give it all for Charity's sweet sake.

And never mourn the loss thereby.

This is to *do Better.*

Piers This will I do, and after that?

Deeds The hardest task of all, oh questing soul,

When thou hast earned thy wage

  and given thine alms,

Then comes the Enemy that did thee wrong.

Him must thou utterly and with full heart

Forgive, as thou dost hope for ultimate

Forgiveness for thine own sinful soul.

This, Piers, is to *Do Best.*

Piers Hard is the road I go. But even this

Will I do, do I find Truth at last.

Come, lead me on. I would not linger now

But set to work, before the daylight ends,

So that the night may come and bring me rest.

SCENE 4

Scene—Piers *and* Do Well

Do Well (*calling*)   How are you doing, Piers, is the work done?

Piers (*in overalls, weary*)   Ay, master, it is, an acre well and truly

ploughed.

Do Well   I have seen it, Piers, the furrows lie deep

and straight, the soil is well turned over, it will make

good growing land. You have done well. Here is full

wage for a day's work.

Piers   And right glad I am to have it. (*Yawning.*)

My limbs are heavy and my back aches, and I am
hungry indeed. I am content to have earned my
supper and a night's rest.

Do Well   Good night, good Piers, sweet sleep attend you!

Piers   Good night, Do Well, you are an honest master.

(*Sits down and opens pack and takes out food.*)

At last! (*Begins to eat a bit of bread.*)

(*Enter a poor Woman with two children, a baby in her arms.*)

Woman   Good evening, Piers!

Piers   Good evening, Friend!

Woman   I pray you pity me and these poor children here. We
have no food, and no money to buy any. I beg for
your help, for Our Dear Lady's sake!

Piers   But I have very little; see this is all I earned by a day's hard labor! (*Puts out his hand.*)

Woman   But we have nothing!

First Child (*crying*)   I am so hungry! O, give me something!!

Second Child   A little piece, I beg. I am hungry, too!

First Child   Mother, I can go no farther, I am so cold and tired.

Second Child   I want some bread, I do! I do!

Piers   (*giving them the food and drink*)

Indeed, you shall have the food, these babes must be fed, and here, take this—

(*hands his bag of wages*)

—and find rest and shelter for you and these little ones.

(*They sit down by Piers and he feeds them.*)

Woman   The Saints reward you, Piers, and sweet Charity, too! You have given your all, and are as poor as I. No man can do better than that! To take all that he hath and give to the poor. Heaven bless you, Pilgrim Piers! Come, children!

Children   Farewell, Piers!

Piers   (*strapping on the empty pack and taking his staff*)

Ah me, I must once more take the road. The journey is a long and painful one, and I am sore minded to despair.

(*Enter* Enemy. *Seeing* Piers, *turns his back and tries to run away.*)

Piers   What's this? Who are you that turn your back on me?

Enemy   (*turning*) You know me, Piers, shouldn't I be afraid of you?

(*Trembles and feels for his sword.*)

Our quarrel is not finished and I am ready now.

Piers (*half draws his sword, but then replaces it.*)

Put away your sword! Since our last encounter, Enemy, I have learned much. I am a Pilgrim now in search of Truth and no falling out must delay me on that road. You did me grievous wrong, but that wrong I do with a full heart, forgive; knowing that we are all but sinful men and temptation besets us all most sorely. Come, give me your hand! Let us be friends once more. Shall it be so?

Enemy (*kneeling at* Piers's *feet*)   You forgive me?! Piers, I am guilty! I am a traitor! I acknowledge my sin. And your forgiveness comes as sweet balm to my soul, for I have been an unhappy man. Piers, you have won in the fight and confounded me utterly, for this is the best that man can do, forgive the injury that a guilty man has done to an innocent one.

Piers   It is forgiven and we are both free men again. Come, give me your hand, we are brothers indeed.

SCENE 5

Scene—Before the locked door of the House of Truth. Soft music throughout scene till Truth's *speech.*

Purity	Come, look everyone, who is this that comes? Far in the distance. It is Pilgrim Piers.
Humility	With bowed head he walks, and faltering step As if he were fearful of the journey's end.
Courage	No, see, he lifts his head full high As one who knows that victory is sure.
Content	He smiles as if he has nothing left to wish, Content to rest after the long day's strife.
Temperance	All gifts he has used well and now is here To lay them at the feet of Truth he sought.
Charity	The flame of love is burning on his brow. And burns for ever, love can never die.

Peace   In his soul the quiet of God's sending,

A blessing, Pilgrim Piers, at the day's ending.

(*Enter* Piers *and* Hope)

Piers (*blindfolded*) The road is very dark that I must tread.

Mine eyes are holding still with thoughts of earth,

With sin, and evil deeds that I have done.

And all the crowding shapes of the vain world

That I would like to forget. Sweet Hope, I pray

Take off this bandage, let me see the light.

Hope   The journey is just about done, and Pilgrim Piers,

A full-grown man and yet a little child,

Can enter here. Come, Innocence, undo

The bandage that obscures his sight and give

To him the key that can unlock the door.

Innocence (*a child*)   (*undoes bandage*) Piers, thou art free, and here the
golden key.

Piers   The end at last! (*Undoes the door, there is music, etc.*)

(Truth *seated on a throne with two servants on either side,*

holding a palm and a crown.)

Truth   Welcome, Ploughman Piers,

Through much tribulation doth the pilgrim come

To find at last the dear abode of Truth.

'Tis truth that fills the empty heart of man

With richness of her splendid dower;

'Tis she who holds the mystic lamp on high,

The lamp of wisdom, love and high endeavor,

And saves the humble soul that seeketh her

With single aim and service free.

Your doubting heart has found its answer now

And rests at ease with all its wandering done.

The task is o'er; here, pilgrim, take the palm,

Take here the crown, it is the great reward

Which nobly beyond death proclaims the end.

SONG OF WELCOME

Forget the weary days,

Over the stony ways,

Gone are the sun's fierce rays.

Hail, Pilgrim! Hail!

Forget the bitter wind,

The scorn of men unkind,

The earthly snares that bind.

Hail, Pilgrim! Hail!

Loosed is the heavy chain,

The weariness and pain,

The enemy is slain.

Hail, Pilgrim! Hail!

Welcome the breaking dawn

Out of the black night torn

Into this glory born.

Hail, Pilgrim! Hail!

Well has thou earned the palm

After long strife the calm.

Sing we with chant and psalm.

Hail, Pilgrim! Hail!

Thou art by fair Truth crowned,

Worthy and true art found,

Let now the song resound,

Hail, Pilgrim! Hail!

Hail, Pilgrim! Hail to thee!

Sing we with melody.

Voices in harmony,

Hail, Pilgrim! Hail!

EPILOGUE

Will Langland *speaks.*

And now these children here have played their part

And like poor Pilgrim Piers have reached the end

Of their long cherished dream, that you, their friends,

Should see them re-create this tale of mine.

It is no story of a bygone day.

Piers wanders still, haunting the hearts of men,

Hating the ill that seeks to overwhelm

The soul. The rich today have wronged the poor.

High places, honor, fame, are bought and sold.

Mothers toil and children weep, and Piers still asks,

"Where does Truth dwell?" One brief moment and I

Thought that she was here, and my mad wandering Will

Might know my doubting Piers had found the goal

Of his long quest. If this be so, no gulf

Divides us through the long deep sleep of time,

But that May morning on the Malvern Hills

Melts to this dark December eve, as dawn

Passes through light to darkness and the dark

Gives place to dawn again. Alas, we must part

Tonight. I, Will Langland, a poor poet still,

These children of today their future yet untried,

And you, our friends. To all my thanks are due

Who made my ancient vision for one moment true.

THE END

THE THREE KINGS

Dramatis Personae

Messenger (Pedro)

Court Music Master (Señor Rocca)

The Queen of Spain

Three Courtiers (One named Don Pedro, one is a Duke)

Philip, Grandson of Louis XIV France

Joseph, Son of Elector of Bavaria, Bavaria

Charles, Son of Emperor Leopold, Austria

The Court Lawyer (aka Don Henrico, aka Señor Abadago)

The Court Lawyer's Assistant

The Papal Nuncio (aka Papal Legate)

Philip's Advocate/Lawyer

Joseph's Advocate/Lawyer

Charles's Advocate/Lawyer

Philip's Servant/Herald

Joseph's Servant/Herald

Charles's Servant/Herald

Governess to the Queen's Household (Señora)

Children

    Andrea

    Sebastian

    Iago

    Juan

    Francesco

    Nita

    Carlos

    Dolores

    Maria

The Peasant Women

Servant

Señora Antonia Olivera

Baby Carlos

(Found among the poems Frances wrote in the British Library is this introduction to this play. A narrator would have read it as a prologue.—Ed.)

At Christmas time in Spain, the Three Kings ride

Down every street, up every wayside lane

Bearing their gifts and journeying far and wide

From barest mountain to the laughing plain.

And ere they come the little children set

Water and fodder and a bed of hay

That tired beasts may for a while forget

Hunger and thirst and the long dangerous way.

Such children have their presents from the Kings

Passing from Spain to Bethlehem.

At Christmas time—the hour of little things

The Kings reward those who remembered them.

Such is the Legend, and our little play

Would mix a legend with some history

And from the cold facts of a bygone day

Would wrest and hold the childish mystery.

We crave your kind indulgence once again

For this attempt to set upon the stage

A story of Three Kings who tried to reign

Whose lives are written in a nation's page.

And of those other Kings who sought a King

And found Him—and were very, very wise,

For like the child, they saw the amazing thing

Through the strange knowledge in his wondering eyes.

And try to show a very simple guise

How a child's faith may bring to life a thing

That now is hid from prudent and from wise

So from the seed may come the blossoming.

ACT 1

Scene—A music room in the Palace

Messenger	Her Majesty bids me tell you she is prepared to hear the Court Children play this afternoon at four o'clock precisely.
Music Master	Dear me, dear me, is that so? It is very alarming and very gratifying that Her Majesty should deign to listen to the efforts of these children. I pray they may do justice to the occasion.
Messenger	Her Majesty is tender-hearted.
Music Master	True. I need not fear too much; and who knows, the children's music may serve to lighten her sad heart. Since the death of the King, God rest his soul (*crosses himself*) she has scarcely smiled. 'Tis a heavy burden that she bears. The weight of this vast kingdom upon her woman's shoulders and none to help. If her son had been spared, God rest his soul, (*crosses himself again*) all might have been well. But time draws on. Good Pedro, summon the children and bid them bring their instruments of music. And moreover let some be prepared to dance before the Queen. She is a true Spaniard and loves the dance.
Messenger	I don't doubt she will be gracious. I'll call your young musicians.

(*Goes out.*)

Music Master (*Fussily preparing the room*)

The triangles must be here, and here, the tambourines, and the violins not too far forward. The music is in sad disorder (*sorting it*) but the children know it well. Little Sebastian is an able conductor, but Carlos is uncertain in his leads sometimes; but there, there, they are very young, and Her Majesty is tender hearted. Here they come.

(*Enter children, each bows to the Master, who points out their places.*)

Music Master   Now quietly, quietly. You are to play before the Queen and my pupils must do poor Maestro Rocca justice, for he has worked hard to teach the little hands to play and the little ears to hear exactly…

(*They play part of 2 short pieces, a scherzo and a rondo.*)

Music Master   And they shall also dance…

Now patience, till Her Majesty shall come

(*a little whispering and fidgeting and tuning up noises.*)

Messenger   Her Majesty.

(*Enter Queen and two or three courtiers—the Children all bow*)

Queen   So, Maestro Rocca, you and your orchestra are all prepared?

Music Master   Your Majesty—yes. The children of your Court are diligent pupils, and now are happy you should hear what they can do. It is little, perhaps, but they desire to please you.

Queen   It is well, no man can do more. What will they play?

Music Master A scherzo, a rondeau, and a dance, your Majesty.

Queen A good selection indeed. Let them begin.

(*The children play the scherzo.*)

Queen That was well done. And now for the rondeau. Your little daughter did excellently, Don Pedro.

Don Pedro (*one of her courtiers*) Thank you, Your Majesty. She is a good student and good Señor Rocca takes an infinity of trouble.

Queen Indeed he does. Let the orchestra play the Rondeau, Señor.

Music Master With the greatest of pleasure, Your Majesty. Come, Sebastian, call your players to attention.

Sebastian It is a difficult piece, Señor, but I will do my best.

Music Master So, so, last week it went very well.

(*The children play the rondeau.*)

Queen That was even better! I want to thank your youthful conductor. Come here, Sebastian (*he advances and bows*). Study carefully and well, and who knows but that you will make and write music when you are a grown man. Is that all Señor?

Music Master The children would like to ask your Majesty's permission to dance a….

Queen I have no heart for dancing, but I do love to see the children dance…In spite of all her sorrows, Spain will dance. Is that not so, Duke?

Duke   Indeed that is true, and may it ever continue to be
            so. There is all poetry and all music in a dance.

Queen   A dance then—

(Orchestra plays and children dance.)

            Indeed it is a pretty sight. Come and let me thank
            the little dancers.

(They advance and bow and courtesy to the Queen.)

            They have let me forget my troubles for a moment.
            But now I must leave, for there are grave matters at
            hand. Adios, Señor—adios Niños.

(The Queen exits with her courtiers; Señora enters)

Music Master Now clear the room and put the music straight and I
            will leave you to the care of Señora here, who will
            look after you well. This evening we must have
            another practice, for it is almost Christmas and there
            is the Christmas music to be studied, and especially
            the March of the Kings, which is far from perfect.
            Adios—adios.

Señora   Adios, Maestro. *(He leaves.)* Come children, let
            everything be in order, and then you can play and
            talk until practice time.

(She sits and sews and the children make a group around her.)

            You will have hard work with the Christmas music,
            for there are but two days left till the Kings come.

Andrea   It is too true—the three Kings pass this way. But we may be asleep and never see them enter by the palace gate.

Sebastian   I will not sleep. I'll keep an open eye and watch from that high window there until they pass beneath the bridge and climb the slope to the great door and ask to come in here.

Iago   They'll bring us presents, won't they? I want a silver sword and a big, big Spanish flag.

Juan   And I'd like a wooden horse, so I can ride.

Francesco   And wooden soldiers, officers, and men. We can have battles then right here on the floor.

Nita   A baby's cradle is what I want most of all, like the one my little brother sleeps in.

Señora   But have you all remembered what to do before the Kings will bring the gifts you ask?

Carlos   We forgot! Oh, pray it's not too late. Come on, Juan, help me, we must get some hay, some straw and some water.

         (*Carlos and Juan go out.*)

Maria   What are they doing? Why do they want hay?

Sebastian   Because when the Kings arrive with all their train of servants, their horses, mules and camels, all will look for food and sweet smelling hay and straw to lie on and cool water to drink after the long and dusty road that they traveled on in order to find the Holy Child.

Dolores   Yes, they bring their presents to our little Lord and some for us, if we remember well to leave provision for the tired beasts.

Señora   Yes, that is so, now all must give a hand. Carlos and Juan are coming with the hay.

(*Enter* Carlos *and* Juan.)

Carlos   It's such a heavy load, but there may be a crowd of horses, mules and camels, too.

Iago   Come on, let's spread it out, there'll be room for them all I think.

Nita   Here's a soft bed, in case they bring a dog.

Andrea   Oh, how I'd love to see the Kings arrive, 'twould be a wondrous sight—silver and gold—their gifts, and gold, frankincense and myrrh.

Señora   Well, who knows, perhaps you'll have your wish.

(*Smiles, significantly.*)

Francesco   (*Looking out of the window.*)   Why see those horses there upon the hill, and the train of mules and such a crowd of men.

Sebastian   And one is riding on a milk-white steed.

Juan   Let me look, too. Oh! one rides a coal black horse.

Nita   (*Crowding at the window.*) And a third is drawing near the gate, and he rides a lovely roan. Who can they be?

Dolores   Don't you know? Can't you see? They are the Kings who come to greet the Holy Child.

Carlos   But is He here? I thought He would be found at Bethlehem.

Señora   He is here, too, wherever loving children are, He makes his home.

Maria   (*Whispering to Nita.*)   These are the Kings, I know;

They've come from far away, and somewhere near to us they'll find the Little Lord. We must be patient and wait till darkness comes.

Carlos   See! See, they are riding now across the bridge; how grand they look—like pictures in a book.

Sebastian   They've reached the palace door and have to stoop their heads so they can enter in.

Señora   Just as the Kings of old, at Bethlehem's tiny door. I fear these have as homage in *their* hearts only greed of gold, and power, and earthly thrones they covet sorely. This poor distracted land that has no King must wait while envious men talk and fight and plead who has the greatest right to reign as King when our loved Queen shall leave the world that has been but a sorry home for her.

Iago   Now all have disappeared and it is dark. Only one little lantern still shines bright under the palace door.

Francesco   But they have brought our gifts and when the sun shines in the sky we shall find them safe.

Andrea	Yes, that is so, but I fear I shall not sleep, I want to see the Kings.
Dolores	And so do I, but I am tired and can hardly keep awake.
Señora	Well, here comes Señor Rocca and he will let you go, when you have sung your song.
Music Master	Indeed you shall, but before you say good night, I want to hear you sing the Christmas song of the Three Kings, and then rest and sleep for tired babes. Come all—one, two, one, two…

CAROL OF THE KINGS

Three Kings rode from East and West,

Caspar, Balthazar and Melchior,

They followed a star that blazed o'erhead

Miles upon miles had they been led

To see a Child in the lowly bed,

As a swallow in a nest.

Three Kings spoke as they rode their way,

Caspar, Balthazar and Melchior,

"Are the caskets safe that hide the gold,

Incense and myrrh; do the frail clasps hold?

For these in Solomon's days were old,

Usage and rust betray."

"The locks are sound, the gifts secure,

Caspar, Balthazar and Melchior,

Sealed were they in a land afar

When ye went forth to follow a star,

To find the greatest of things that are,

The Son of a Virgin pure.

Mary will know the gifts you bring,

Caspar, Balthazar and Melchior,

Mary will keep your gold apart,

Mary who did keep things in her heart,

Things that gladden and things that smart;

Will hold these for a King."

The Three Kings answered, "Yes, we bear,

Caspar, Balthazar and Melchior,

Gold for a King, incense for Priest,

Myrrh for a death, for that at least

Three Kings journeyed out of the East

To see a stable bare.

Ah, Mary! take the gifts we lay,

Caspar, Balthazar and Melchior.

Low at His feet, His tiny feet

That shall walk the plain, the sea, the street;"

And Mary smiled, with a smile so sweet,

At the young Child in the hay.

ACT 2

SCENE—The Audience Chamber in the Palace

Court Servants

(preparing the throne, etc.)

1ˢᵗ Servant   The audience is set for midday when her Majesty returns from Mass.

2nd Servant	That is so. The princes and their advocates and servants wait in the great hall till they are summoned here.
1st Servant	The Papal Legate has already spoken with Her Majesty and the Crown Lawyers have been in conference since early dawn.
2nd Servant	It's a bad thing when there is no heir to a great kingdom like ours. Who can tell whether the choice shall fall upon the right head or not?

(*Enter the* Court Lawyer.)

Court Lawyer	Is everything prepared?

(*Looks out of the window.*)

	Her Majesty is already crossing the Great Court.
1st Servant	Everything is prepared.
2nd Servant	A messenger is waiting.
Court Lawyer	It is well—there must be no delays. The matter is urgent.
Messenger	Her Majesty and Papal Legate. (*They enter.*)

(*Court Lawyer bows and kisses the Queen's hand.*)

Queen	Ah, Señor Abadago, you have a difficult task; to listen and to judge the cause of each of these three royal princes who each want to claim the throne when I am gone from this world.

Court Lawyer	It is indeed a grave business your Majesty, and needs much discretion and patience; but with the help of Holy Church I pray we may be rightly guided in this matter.
Queen	Indeed, I pray we may. For me, I am wearied to death and only crave to have the question settled. Sorrow has fallen heavily upon me. To lose husband and son in three short years. The king was old but the prince was young, and I never saw his death coming. But in battle who can tell? The one is taken, and the other left. It is all a mystery.
Papal Legate	But he died for Spain, your Majesty; this must be your comfort.
Queen	It is my only comfort, but I am all alone; had there been but a child, Spain would not then be at the mercy of these strangers. But I must cease to mourn. Let the princes be called to audience.
Messenger	I will summon them, your Majesty.
Court Lawyer	I have studied the claims as you have done, Reverend Father, have you formed any decision?
Papal Legate	None at all. Nor will I till I have heard the learned advocates who will each plead the claim of their august clients.
Messenger	The princes await an audience.
Queen	Let them advance.

(*Enter three* Heralds *and three* Princes)

Philip's Herald   Philip, Duke of Aujon, son of the Dauphin,
grandson of Louis the XIV, the King of France.

(*He bows and kisses the Queen's hand, and he and his advocate take
their seats.*)

Joseph's Herald Prince Joseph Ferdinand of Bavaria.

(*He bows and kisses the Queen's hand and takes a seat with his
advocate.*)

Charles's Herald The Archduke Charles of Austria.

(*He bows and kisses the Queen's hand, and takes his seat with his
lawyer/advocate.*)

(*Lawyers sit around a table in front, the claimants/Princes sit towards
the back.*)

Court Lawyer   The royal princes are assembled. It is well that we
should hear the claim of each. Begin Señor Abadago,
if you please. By what right does your master, Prince
Philip of France, claim the throne of Spain?

Philip's Lawyer (*Opens a small casket containing parchment.*)

By this indisputable claim, Don Henrico, about
which there should be neither question nor
controversy.

Court Lawyer's Assistant

Proceed Señor Abadago.

Philip's Lawyer When your great king, Charles II, and her Majesty's royal consort died (God rest his soul) and when his only son perished on the field of battle a few short months ago (God rest **his** soul), my royal master Louis XIV, the Roi Soleil, the Sun King of France, claimed the throne of Spain for his grandson, Philip, who in person here seeks for the due acknowledgment of his right. Our great and glorious monarch had taken to wife the sister of your gallant king whose death we all lament, and she renouncing all claim to the throne of Spain, yet with the knowledge and consent of Charles, your King, should heirs of his body fail, named her grandson, the Dauphin's son, as successor to this crown and kingdom. Through his grandmother's birth my prince is great nephew to your late King, and hereby declares there can be none other with so good a right, seeing it was with the cognizance of his late Majesty that a deed was drawn up appointing him the heir to the throne of Spain, should no true heir be forthcoming to ascend the throne when Her Majesty shall be called upon to surrender all earthly crowns and thrones.

Joseph's Lawyer If there was a secret will made by the King of Spain with the King of France, we do not know of it. It cannot be evidence unless such a will can be produced.

Charles's Lawyer The document must be investigated if such exists, otherwise the claim is but a flimsy pretext and will not hold good in law.

Court Lawyer   The Prince will no doubt submit the will.

Philip   It is here, the proof is in my claim. The will is in safe keeping.

Court Lawyer   We will continue. By what right does the Archduke Charles of Austria a right to the throne of Spain?

Charles's Lawyer

Here is no secret will or treaty. My royal master claims direct decent from your king Philip III. As is well known Philip had a daughter who wedded the Austrian King Ferdinand, and her son Leopold by his second marriage is the father of my lord and heir direct and true to this great kingdom.

Philip's Lawyer   That claim cannot be maintained, for the heir is but a descendant by a second marriage. There is an heir by a first marriage.

Joseph's Lawyer

It is on that ground that I state the claim of my royal client, Joseph Ferdinand.

Charles's Lawyer

But the claim cannot stand for a moment, for——

Court Lawyer   Señores, silence if you please. We must hear what the Prince Joseph Ferdinand has to state.

Joseph's Lawyer

None has so clear a claim as my Prince here, and the

house of Bavaria is ever at one with the house of Spain. My master is a grandson of that same Leopold whose son the Archduke Charles has already made his claim. But see Señores, by what much clearer right he asks your consideration. By his grandfather's first marriage with your own Spanish Princess Margaret Theresa, whose daughter Maria is this Prince Joseph Ferdinand's mother. The case is clear and the line of succession direct, and my prince demands that his claim be duly conceded and acknowledged.

Court Lawyer   There can be no question of demand, Señor— the question is one for the deepest consideration. Her Majesty must be allowed to examine such a claim on its own merits.

Queen   Señores, I have no choice in this grave matter. I can but leave the decision to the lawyers here, whose business it will be to report upon the result of their investigation. I pray God may guide their labors.

Court Lawyer   Your Majesty speaks true; the matter is so grave a one that there can be no hasty decision.

Court Lawyer's Assistant

We shall call for further explanations than these first claims that have been placed before us.

Court Lawyer   Yes, and it would be well that the Princes themselves should enter into discussion, as well as their advocates.

Philip   Only too gladly. Señor Abadago, my lawyer has put the case well, and there is no doubt that his late Majesty before his lamented death signified his intentions with regard to his great country's future king when he made a will appointing me to succeed, with the full approval and knowledge of His Majesty, my grandfather, Louis XIV of France.

Joseph   That will must be forthcoming.

Charles   Yes—evidence, evidence.

Philip   Is not my word enough?

Charles   Certainly not!.

Joseph   This is no paltry affair for lawyers to quibble and trifle, but it is the destiny of a great nation; therefore all cards must be upon the table and the will produced. Will you demand that Señor Abadago— Don Henrico?

Court Lawyer   In good time, Señores.

Papal Legate   (*Aside to* Court Lawyer.)

The will is in safe keeping.

Charles   Why does the Legate whisper to Don Henrico? There is some treachery here.

Joseph   I demand that my claim be at once conceded, or I take the sword in defense of my rights.

Papal Legate   There is no question of swords Prince Joseph—
                    you are young and hot-headed.

Charles   No, Joseph is in the right. I, too, would defend
                    my cause with guns and swords upon the
                    battlefield.

Philip   And I shall not hesitate either if it comes to
                    that.

Papal Legate   Be careful, Señores, war is easily begun and with
                    difficulty ended.

Court Lawyer   This is a matter for advocates—for lawyers—
                    and as such I and my colleagues are prepared to
                    consider the claims of each.

Queen   Your Highnesses, I pray there be no quarreling
                    among you. Surely this matter may be settled
                    peaceably.

Court Lawyer   I would remind your Majesty that when all the
                    questions raised have been weighed and
                    judgment pronounced, it will be our duty to
                    urge your Majesty to make a will that shall
                    clearly leave this throne to him who has the
                    greatest right.

Queen   Must it indeed finally rest with me? In
                    mourning and saddened, why must I decide?

Papal Legate   Having been called to this great office, your
                    Majesty must indeed fulfill the obligations of it.

Joseph's Lawyer There will be no other course of action, and when the claims of these princes have been more carefully considered, the lawyers of your court will present their considered judgment.

Philip's Lawyer Let there be no delay. I am in no mood to hang about while these men talk and argue.

Charles There is no need for further consideration. I defy anyone to dispute my claim.

Joseph A rightful decision, Señores. And what do I care? The sword shall decide.

Philip A decision in arms. Then indeed the case is settled. France will not fail!

Charles Don't be too sure, Prince Philip. Austria is mighty in arms.

Joseph Not greater than the lion of Bavaria, that will take no note of French lilies or Austrian eagle.

Queen Princes, I beg of you, let there be no disputing here. We are almost to Christmas, and there should be nothing but peace and goodwill among men.

Papal Legate A good reminder, your Majesty, and we should well observe it.

Joseph There will only be peace when my true claim is acknowledged.

Philip Then there will never be peace as your claim is fantastic.

Charles Let her Royal Highness decide right now! And then

	we can keep our Christmas in our own lands. As Archduke of Austria and King of Spain, mine will be the merriest feast of all!
Queen	Ah! Señores—Señores, how shall I decide? Pray you be patient with me.
Philip	Until tomorrow, Madam.
Charles	Tonight, I say! Tonight!
Joseph	Before we leave this Council Chamber!
Papal Legate	This is unseemly—you cannot force her Majesty thus.
Court Lawyer	Her Majesty's decision shall be given.
Joseph	Now!
Philip	Yes, now!
Charles	Why should I wait?

(*A loud knock at the door.*)

| **Court Lawyer** | Who comes to interrupt—see who knocks. |

(Messenger *ushering in a* Court Servant.)

Queen	Well, what is it?
Servant	Your Majesty—a woman is waiting outside, who desires audience, but I have told her it is impossible.
Court Lawyer	Bid her be gone—her business can wait.

Servant	She says it cannot wait—it concerns the matter on which her Majesty is now engaged.
Queen	How can that be?
Servant	I do not know your Majesty, but she is most urgent, and stands there weeping and begs your Majesty to receive her before it is too late.
Papal Legate	Too late—too late for what?
Court Lawyer	What could this woman know of the business at hand?
Philip	Are we to dangle about here while a woman asks audience? Attend to your case Señor Abadago.
Philip's Lawyer	Let us continue. His Highness would have things settled…
Joseph	Yes, bid the woman be off.
Queen	It is I, Prince Joseph, who give orders in this house. Bid the woman enter.
Charles	This is monstrous! A State Council interrupted because a woman wants a petticoat!
Papal Legate	(*to* Charles)
	No, your Highness, she may need help for her husband, brother, son—we shall see.
Servant	The woman approaches, your Majesty. Her name is Antonia Olivera.

Court Lawyer   The name is common enough.

Servant (*announces*) Antonia Olivera.

> (*Antonia enters with a child in her arms, looks bewildered at her surroundings, sees the Queen, curtseys awkwardly and then stands trembling.*)

Queen   What is it, Antonia? Speak, do not be afraid. Have you business that concerns this Council?

Antonia   Your Majesty, I will try to tell my tale. It is but three days ago I heard in Alagon, near Segovia, your Majesty, where I live—my husband has a little farm and works on the hillside, and Alagon is the market town…

Queen   I know—proceed Antonia—what did you hear in Alagon?

Philip   What nonsense is this?

Joseph   Never deal with women, they're impossible.

Charles   I am leaving the Council (*half rises*).

Charles's Lawyer

  No—I beg your Royal Highness—that would be a grave error.

Antonia   I heard that your Majesty must make a will so that this country may have a King to rule when your Majesty should die, and when I heard that I knew what I must do. I must bring the King that is to be to his own Palace.

163

(Holds out the baby.)

Court Lawyer Are you mad? I pray your Majesty send the woman
away.

Queen Let me hear further, Antonia. What do you mean,
"the king that is to be"?

Antonia Why this is the manner of it your Majesty. It is nigh
a year ago since your son, Prince Carlos, came to
Alagon. He was sore driven by his enemies, but in
Alagon we were faithful, and for the space of three
months we guarded him well, I and my husband and
my daughter Maria. She was beautiful and good your
Majesty, and how shall I say it? He a Prince of Royal
Blood of Spain loved her and wedded her in the
little Church of Santa Lucia. Here are the proofs
your Majesty. He knew he would never reign as
King, but he bade her keep them safe.

Joseph This is some monstrous lie.

Charles A tale to tell the children.

Queen Give me the papers.

(Hands them to the Court Lawyer.)

Look well into this Señor Abadago. Continue, Antonia.

Antonia Twice he returned, your Majesty, and on his second
visit, his little son was three days old. He sent for the
priest and the babe was baptized Carlos, too, your
Majesty. Here are the papers and the letter he wrote
your Majesty, commending his wife and son to your

care. (*Gives letter.*)

Queen   It is his letter, it is his handwriting! My son—my son.

Charles   A plot—a plot.

Queen   And his mother, Antonia?

Antonia (*weeping*)

Alas, your Majesty, when she heard of the prince's death upon the field of battle, her grief was too great, and she died, so young, so lovely.

Queen   This woman is speaking the truth, Señores, and God has spoken. Give me the child.

(*Takes him in her arms.*)

(*Addressing Joseph, Philip and Charles as she holds out the child*)
Princes: —The King of Spain!

Curtain

Messenger comes to center stage and reads from a scroll.

Messenger   To Her Royal Highness the Queen of Spain

Revered Sovereign and Beloved Mother,

Since when this letter shall fall into your royal hands I shall be no more, for well I know that I am very near my end, and by certain foretellings that I am to die shortly, where indeed I should fain die upon the field of battle—yet ere that day comes I would commend to your royal care my true wife and my infant son. For indeed Maria Olivera is my beloved wife, wedded to me with all the rites of Holy Church. The proofs are in her keeping to be delivered to you as occasion requires. This infant is in truth my very son Carlos, baptized by the priest at Alagon.

I pray you Madame, my beloved Mother, guard them well, for indeed they are dear to me. Let no man seek to dispute the just claim of my son to the throne of Spain. The time is very short that I must depart hence, so of your charity most beloved mother, pray for the soul of your unworthy son, who leaves his all in your august keeping.

Signed: Carlos Ferdinando

Prince of Spain and Aragon and Castille.

ACT 3

Scene—Ante Room of Audience Chamber

Carlos   *(Alone, searching about.)*

I have searched the palace from the topmost roof
to the cellar underground, from room to room.
The servant's hall, the chapel and the court,
the banquet chamber, the cupboards, searching
everywhere, the stables too, and though I saw the
beasts, horses and mules and even camels there, I never
saw the Kings. I am in despair, I thought I would see
them, though Sebastian said they were not true kings

who came, and Juan thought they'd only passed by here on their way to Bethlehem.

But I know that they are here somewhere. I've never seen **this** room inside before, for the Señora said it was here the Queen gave audiences, and we must not go in. But as the door was open I peeped in, for just possibly they still may come this way. It will take them to the chapel, and I saw the Holy Child asleep in His Mother's arms as I went by Her Majesty's own room. I did not see His face, but He lay still and softly folded in a crimson shawl.

(*Sees table with caskets.*)

But oh! the Kings **have** passed this way, for look! their presents are on the table here—caskets that hold the gold, the frankincense, the myrrh. They will come in here to get these gifts, and I will see their splendor and their humble eyes when they kneel down with offerings to the Little Lord.

(*Sound of voices outside—entering, the Princes all angry and disturbed.*)

They may be angry if they find me here. I'll slip behind this curtain—if they don't know the passage to the chapel, I can show them the way.

Charles   It's all a monstrous plot, hatched by the Queen who thinks by means like this to save the throne from me, the rightful heir.

Joseph   Has a Prince ever been treated so badly, been so betrayed! To give my rights to a bastard child!

Philip   I will not yield, I'd rather the world started a war
than I give up my rights, which no man can dispute.

Joseph   But I **do** dispute your claim, and furthermore, the
claim of the Archduke—and further still, the claim,
so manifestly false, of this same child that has been
foisted on a foolish Queen who has no idea of what
she's doing!

Charles   I'll never surrender my just rights. I've said it is a
plot and a plot it is—the lawyers almost certainly will
prove the papers are forgeries and the tale a lie.

Philip   Then the whole argument begins again with we
three, and I demand, Señores that you give no
further thought to your advancement here.

Charles   No further thought? My lawyer does the work of
thinking—there is no question here for any need of
thought.

Joseph   When this child's claim has finally been proved a
fabrication and a pack of lies, the prince's letter just
a clever scheme to play upon the grieving feelings of
the Queen—the marriage, birth and christening all
found to be a forgery—then Señores both, I will
maintain more strongly than ever that the throne of
Spain is mine by right inalienable, and true, and may
not be contradicted.

Charles   Never I tell you! —Never shall that be!

Philip   We well may have to leave the question now. The throne is mine, I would remind you both.

Joseph   Nothing is proved!

Charles   Never—never I say again!

Carlos   (*peeping through the curtains*)

> Why do they quarrel like this? They are the Kings but perhaps they are tired and need food and rest. They've come a long and weary way, but their journey is ended now.

Charles (*noticing Carlos*)

> Who do we have here? Another child—is he too in the plot?

Philip   What is your name? What are you doing in this room?

Carlos   My name is Carlos.

Joseph   Who sent you here? —you are a very useless spy.

Carlos   I came here by myself. I knew that you would pass along this way to find the Holy Child. Sebastian and I waited up all night to see the Kings, but then you never came, and so I searched all day—I think perhaps you waited, hiding until the little Child was safely housed and warmed and fed, but He is here. I saw him with my own eyes, wrapped up all warmly in a crimson shawl.

Philip   What does he mean? I think this boy is daft, call a servant here—take him off to bed.

Carlos   No, no, it isn't nearly time for bed, though it is dark—look through that window there, and you will see the star that led you here. On Christmas night we wait till that same star is set and there is no more light before we go to bed.

Joseph   There **is** a splendid star—I never saw anything like it.

Carlos   But as you are a **King**, haven't you seen that star before—quite often?

Joseph   A king—why yes, I call myself a king. A would-be king of Spain, that's true.

Carlos   *(to Charles)* And you, you are a king, you came from far to see the Child. You did, didn't you?

Charles *(aside)* To see the child…

           (aloud) that thought never crossed my mind. I too am a king and seek a kingdom here.

Carlos *(to Philip)*   You are the grandest king—the grandest of them all. You must go first, and I will show your Majesty the way.

           (Moves as if to go off.)

Philip   A king before my time, it seems. This child is dreaming—he believes, as Spanish children do, that the Three Kings of old come with gifts to every little child. Princes, we cannot hurt a child who trusts us.

Joseph   I have a boy who loves his father well. He will be sad without me at this hour.

Charles   We'll play his pretty game and follow him;

(*to Carlos*)

lead on young Carlos, take us where you want us to go.

Carlos   It isn't far—across the courtyard there, you'll see the door and lights within are lit.

Charles   It's a cold night, young Sir, so let us get our cloaks.

Philip   I had meant to leave the palace gates before the moon had risen—so I'm prepared for the weather.

Joseph   Señores, our quarrel rests for a while, so that a child's dream may come true.

Carlos   But wait! You've forgotten your gifts for the Baby. The gold, frankincense and myrrh.

(*runs back to the table and gives each one a casket*)

Now walk softly, the Babe may still be sleeping in the crimson shawl.

(*They go out, the child leading them and they reappear before the closed curtain.*)

(*Music*)

Carlos   Now you are here. I'll call my friends—they'll want to see you kneel before the Holy Babe. They've waited a long while, but now they'll be so glad to hear the Kings are present with their gifts.

(*He goes out calling.*)

Sebastian, Juan, Maria, etc., come! But step softly, here, I have a light to show the way. (*leaves stage*)

Joseph   Am I dreaming?

Charles   I will not fail that child.

Philip   To play a king, it is a noble part.

(Carlos *re-enters, leading the others.*)

Carlos   The Kings came after all, and are just waiting to give their presents to our Little Lord.

(*Curtain opens*)

(*The Queen enthroned with the Child on her knee.*)

(*The Kings look at the Child, and one by one, they pass in front of the throne and lay their claims at the Queen's feet, then pass off in silence, the children are all kneeling.*)

Carlos   So when the great star shone the Three Kings came and paid their homage with their golden gifts and all the children saw them as they knelt, and all their visions of the Kings are true.

Queen   Indeed, yes, it's true. A Child is born to us. We who sorrowed in the night—at dawn, now we see the rising sun and hear the song of birds and angels, mingled so among the strife and noises of the laboring earth that warring men will honor the new birth.

An earthly king has come into his own.

The King of Heaven sits upon his throne, his throne of refuge in a woman's arms.

Arms very much like mine, as sanctuaries from harm, that hold a whole world's joy—

Come, children, all.

A hymn of welcome, before the curtain falls, for an earthly prince, and then the song that brings a greater welcome for the King of Kings.

(All sing a song of welcome, such as O Come All Ye Faithful.)

THE END

The stronger and wiser men grow, the less they are superior to anything.

—Frances Chesterton

Legends of Gods and Saints

(Incomplete)

Children

    Borus

    Dea

    Octo

    Hector

    Ena

    Vesta

    Ion

    Ianthe

    Gadis

    Mona

Principal Child

Other Children

Woman #1

Woman #2

Vulcan

St. Dunstan

Orpheus

St. Cecilia

Diana

St. Joan

Pan

St. Francis

1st Rabbit

2nd Rabbit

3rd Rabbit

Mars

St. George

Scene 1

About ten children playing ball, boys and girls.

Borus   Let's have a rest. I'm tired of foolish games. Sit on the ground and someone tell a tale.

Dea   My mother told me *such* a tale last night.

Octo   What was it all about? Come on, tell us, please! I like your stories Dea, is this a new one?

Dea   It's about the wood gods and the goat god, Pan. And how the great Apollo rode the sun…

Hector (*interrupting*)   My father told me once there was a god in every stream, in every tree and high on Mount Olympus lived the mighty ones who made the earth, the sea, and sky. But they, he said, care nothing for little children now.

Ena   My mother said the gods were dead and we could never find them, even if we searched all day.

Vesta   It's very sad, I love to think that in those trees
(*pointing*) there might be lovely Dryads crowned with bright leaves and laughing all the time.

Ion   I know it's just a tale, but once Proserpine gathered the flowers here and Pluto came and bore her right away into the dark.

Ianthe   Well, let Dea tell her tale. Maybe it's something other than these ones of gods who are all dead.

Child   No, no!

Gadis   Of course, they're dead, you've never seen a god, nor a wood nymph, dryad, philomele, nor Jove, nor Juno, nor Cyclops with one eye.

Mona   Nor Flora, nor Diana with her bow, nor lovely Venus and the little Cupid boy.

Hector   They're only stories, though I wish they could be true.

Child   I'm sure they're true.

Borus   Of course they're only legends that our fathers tell, though very well they know the gods are dead.

Dea   I love the tale of Pan and how he blows his pipes made out of reeds, such lovely tunes. I've often listened there by the riverside, but never heard a sound.

Ion   I've listened too, but only heard the reeds rustling and the wild birds splashing by the lake.

Octo   I wish you'd tell the tale whether it's true or not. Come, Dea, what *was* the story that you said your mother told you?

Dea   Well, you've all heard of Echo, a fair nymph.

Gadis   Echo. Echo—she's not any nymph. But just sound, that travels back again when you call loud in some great lonely place or on the mountains.

Hector   It often sounds as if a spirit answered back. Perhaps a god—

Borus	I tell you all, it was a foolish tale. There are no gods for all the gods are dead.
Child	No, no, I know they are not dead. They sleep, perchance, or hide and wait for us to come and call them from the sky or sea or cave. From out of the trees or from the riverside, they must be there. I often feel that they are just asleep and if I call they'd come.
Ina	I feel like that, but then my mother said there were no gods and what she says is true.
Borus	My father says the same, the gods are dead.
Child	And yet I know they live.
Vesta	If that were only true, how glad I'd be. I'd dance for joy and sing and laugh all day.

Several children together: And so would we!

Gadis	Well you can sing and laugh and dance without the gods. I tell you they are all dead.
Hector	Alas it's no good hoping; they **are** dead.
Mona	Well never mind, let's play again and then we shall forget whether they're dead or not.
Child	And I, who know they live, am going away over the hills and I shall find them yet. And I shall come again and call you all to see the gods that you all said were dead.
Dea	You cannot go alone; you might get killed.

Child   The gods are there, they will not let me die.

Borus   Oh let him go. He'll soon be back and then perhaps he will believe us that the gods are dead.

Child   That I never will believe. And I shall go and search and search until I see them plain and all the tales you tell will all come true. I know that in the very heart of things they live and that we do not see them now because we never look. But I will look and when I've gone a long and lonely way far from you all and cannot hear you say, "The gods are dead" I shall find them there and then I will come back and they with me. And you shall see that those you thought were dead live on and that they were not idle tales you told, but true forever. And how glad, how splendid when that great day comes. I tighten my sandals and take my cloak. And so farewell, farewell. I will return. (*Goes off.*)

Ianthe   I wish he had not gone, he's very young. And he'll be lonely when darkness comes.

Gadis   Oh, never fear, we'll see him soon again. And he'll believe us then. He is too young to understand.

Dea   I cannot tell my story now. I feel too sad. I wish I would have gone with him.

Hector   We've sat here long enough. Come, let's dance. I'm always happy if I can only dance.

Borus   So am I.

Ina   And I.

Vesta   And I. (*They dance.*)

(*Enter two women.*)

1ˢᵗ Woman   Stop children. See the sun has set, and the moon is rising over Dian's Hill. The night is almost here.

2ⁿᵈ Woman   Yes, and it's time for supper, and then for sleep. Away, away, leave the games and dancing till the daylight comes again. Come, children, come.

(*They all exit.*)

EPISODE 1

Child, Vulcan, St. Dunstan

Child   I have come a long, long way, by roughest paths, through darkest woods and by many a stream. And I have searched in every place and called the gods to answer and never heard a sound, nor seen a face. And I am well nigh dead...I can go no further...I am weary...I must sleep...

(*stumbles over Vulcan's bellows*).

What can this be...a blacksmith's forge?

Vulcan   It is.

Child   And who are you?

Vulcan   Don't you know? Haven't you heard the tale of how
I fell from heaven to earth and so I became lame
and every since then I limp as I go along?

Child   Why, you're Vulcan, and I **have** found a god after
all. It was not just a story!

Vulcan   Alas! I don't know. Sometimes I think to myself that
it was all a dream, that I could make great fires on
my forge here. And mighty flames would leap and I
could create metal things any way I wanted to. But now,
my bellows blows for nothing, no fire will rise. It is dead
cold, and I am colder still. My work is done. Men do not
need the lovely things I made with these brave pincers
here.

Child   No, let me try to blow, perhaps the flame will come.

(*tries the bellows*).

    No, I can't, it's so cold. Please—you try again, once
more. I love to see the dancing sparks and hear the
hammer ring.

Vulcan   Child, it is useless. There is no life in it. Cold ashes, and
no answering glow to warm an icy heart. My work is
done. Vulcan will sleep his last deep sleep here at the
foot of his forge that he loved so well.

Child (*crying*) Oh, poor Vulcan, who will help him now? There is no
fire, and he may die of cold.

Dunstan   Why are you crying, child? What is this all about?

Child   Vulcan will die, we cannot light the flame on the forge.

He cannot make the gates of gold, the lovely thrones, the chains, the rings or anything. See here are his hammer and his pincers, see?

Dunstan   Pincers, well I had pincers, too, and plucked the devil by the nose! All red hot my pincers were, and I held him till he cried for mercy! So! If Vulcan made things of brass and gold, he will make them again and with my help, for I can work metal, too. Child, he will hear the sweet bells ring and the organ roll its mighty music in the pipes we make together. Give me the bellows.

(He *blows till light appears.*)

See! the answering light! The flames will leap and the great anvil will roar.

Child   Vulcan, wake up! See, see the light has come.

Vulcan   How can that be? I thought the fire was dead.

Dunstan   I am Saint Dunstan, and I too work a forge. See I can save your wondrous works of old. I need your mighty gates and your circles of gold. For me you'll make thrones and chains to glorify the House of God which is where I come from, I am His servant, and rule this little land. Brother, nothing is lost, live again in me. This child of faith will know the gods don't die, but live forever in a world made new.

Episode Two

Orpheus with lyre of which strings are broken, seated, trying very hard to make music.

Orpheus   The strings are broken, how can I sing now? It was always I since the old days who made music sound so that the birds and bees, the very clouds above even stars in their courses, and the rushing streams stood to listen. Men and women, too, would venture unafraid to see the god whose very notes would stir their hearts right out from their bodies! But, sadly, my music is no more. And Orpheus must weep for glories past, forgotten, lonely, with a broken lyre.

Child (*entering*)   Who is this handsome youth who sits and cries? A music maker but with a harp unstrung and broken notes. Tell me, who are you?

Orpheus   Child, haven't you ever heard of Orpheus? The god, son of the great Apollo, who could charm the beasts, the trees, the mountains themselves with music. But who all his days went sadly mourning Eurydice, whom he loved so well.

Child   You are a god? The gods really aren't dead then?

Orpheus   Not dead, but dying. No one needs them now. No one hears even if Orpheus plays. The lyre is broken, no sound comes from it. I can't sing. My spirit dies within me.

Child   No, no. It can't be. It must not be. Please try once more.

Orpheus (*tries*) You see, there is no sound.

Child   But surely someone knows the proper way to fix the lyre and make the music come out. There! I heard a note!

(*Enter St. Cecilia*)

Cecilia   A broken lyre. (*She picks it up.*) Oh, what a lovely thing.

Child   It is a broken lyre, and here is a broken heart. Orpheus is crying for his lost music.

Cecilia   But music lives forever. I know well for though men may slay me, still the organ rolls. Orpheus, my brother, come look up and smile. I am Cecilia, and I want to sing those songs that made the mountains ring for joy. See I can fix the broken strings and you and I together can make Music pour her very soul into such hymns of praise. Such harmonies to tell of life and death, that men will pause from their work amazed to know that Orpheus plays his lyre once more. Here brother, touch the strings.

Orpheus   I live again, my music is not dead! (*He plays.*)

Cecilia   It lives in me, it is a part of me. Come brother, sing.

Orpheus   Sister, sing with me.

Child   Make lovely music so that I can dance.

SONG

Orpheus:

> The flowers, the birds and the trees
>
> The valleys, the hills and the streams
>
> That have slept a long winter through
>
> Arise from the black mist of dreams.

Cecilia:

> They sing to the glory of God
>
> Who fashioned the spirit of man
>
> To see in the heart of a flower
>
> How his mighty purpose began.

Orpheus:

> Cold earth is warm with the sun
>
> Green is the corn on the hill
>
> The waters untiringly flow
>
> The hurrying rivers to fill.

Cecilia:

They murmur of life and of death

As they rush on their magical way

And of Love that is stronger than death

For death endures but a day.

Orpheus and Cecilia:

The watches of night are gone by

And day in its glory appears

We offer this hymn to thy praise

Oh Father of all of us, hear.

Episode Three

Diana and St. Joan

Diana (*asleep*) (*Enter* Child)

Child   Who is this who sleeps on the cold bare ground? How
              beautiful she is, and oh how sad she looks. Maybe she's
              weary of the chase, she is a hunter—see her quiver lies
              beside her and an unstrung bow. I will sit near and wait
              till she awakens.

Diana (*waking*)   Child, who are you who look with eyes of love on pale Diana, goddess of the night?

Child   You are Diana? Why I've heard my father tell that it was Diana who could climb the sky; who hunted all night in a silver coach drawn by two white stags.

Diana   Child, it was I who climbed up to the vault of the sky and hunted in the realms of space. Hunted till the sky was emptied of the moon and stars were dim jewels of the night. The fierce sun came and drove me to my rest. Now I cannot hunt anymore, men say that I am dead. And the great bow will not bend. Though I try to use all my strength (*tries to bend it*).

The arrows in the bright quiver are useless and don't work in a broken bow. Joy in the chase is gone, and I'll break these arrows as a man might snap a twig from off an old dead tree. (*Breaks an arrow.*)

Child   No, please don't break them, they will be needed soon. See, someone is coming, a warrior it seems. Though truly, the soldier is a girl and it is she who will help to mend the broken bow.

Joan   A girl I am indeed, servant of France who fought beneath the oriflamme— the red banner of St. Denis.

(The red banner of St. Denis.)

And I dared to lead men into a bloody battle when arrows poured like hail out of the sky. Arrows that pierced me as I rode to Paris. I needed arrows then, and many a bow was drawn by many a valiant hand. For that dear land that Joan the maid might save from fire and famine and the endless foe.

Child   And will you fight again? With this bow? It is so useless now.

Joan   Aye, that I will, for evil still does ride the world and often unseen. I lead my men to death and victory in a holy cause. Fair Diana with the unstrung bow and broken shafts: Lift up your head and see. Here where it stands complete and tight with fine arrows fixed and ready for the fray. An arrow is a piece of wood with a bird's strong wing to fly through space and land on the ground. But of two arrows I can make a sign that men will follow to the gates of death (*makes a cross of two arrows.*) And men find joy in following. This was my consolation in that most evil day when I must taste the cruelty of man and the bitterness of death. And so the bow forever must be bent. The arrows pointed that the birds may fly, and hunt unceasingly the souls of men. Sister, come with me, shall not Joan the Maid, whose heart is all aflame with holy fire take cold Diana and so warm her heart that she may burn forever with desire to slay the evil and uphold the right. Come, sister, the hour is nigh at hand.

Child   How they do love each other, and see how beautiful they look. I pray their hunting may be good.

Episode Four

Pan and St. Francis

Pan is seated dejectedly under a tree with animals around him, who try to attract his attention, but in vain.

Enter Child.

Pan   This is a stranger. Who by chance are you that wander near the haunts of the great god Pan?

Child   I am a child, I came from far away to find the gods whom men said were dead.

Pan (*bitterly*)   And they say true. For I am almost dead. I am too tired to live, I and my friends (*points to the animals*) will be content to die.

1ˢᵗ Rabbit   No, no—we want to live and run and play and hide among the ferns up on the hill.

2ⁿᵈ Rabbit   And we come to Pan for food and shelter when we are cold and hungry.

3ʳᵈ Rabbit   Pan is our father, he would never want us to die.

Pan   No, I would not want you to die, but I don't care any more about all the beautiful animals and the fruit and flowers that I once loved. I am too tired to play my pipe of reeds. No one will hear and Pan would pipe in vain. My constant friends, you must go away and find some other help than mine to keep yourselves from harm. Go away, away! Be off I say, be off.

(*Rabbits scuffle off in all directions.*)

Child   What have you done? Oh who will love them now?

Pan   I don't know. And I am going to hide my head and wait for the end, for Pan is dead indeed.

(*Goes out.*)

Child   Oh, I am sad. I would have loved poor Pan and all his little friends. But now, they've no one to care for them. Why has he left them like that? (*Weeps.*)

Francis (*creeps in and sits where Pan sat, in the same attitude. In a moment, the rabbits scuttle back in and seat themselves around him.*)

Child   Why look! The rabbits have come back! And now they rub their soft heads against this stranger's knee. Just like they used to do to Pan! Has he returned in some sort of disguise? He looks both kind and sad. I will go closer—I don't feel afraid.

(*He seats himself hear to St. Francis who lays his hand upon the child's head.*)

Are you a god? I thought that Pan had gone. These were his friends. Stranger, are you Pan?

Francis   Child, I am one who through long years of pain with poverty and obedience as my guides, have with my poor Franciscans tramped the globe. We keep the holy things secure so that men may find safe refuge from the storms that beat upon the fortress of their souls. When I was but a lad, how happy I was! How I would dress in silk and rare colors. I'd eat and drink whatever pleased me. I'd laugh out in the streets, or on the wide plains of Italy. And now you see, this rough robe is my dress. And bread and water will be my complete meal, and I'll be content. And men have named me almost with a laugh: Little poor man.

Child   How did it all happen? How did you get such a name?

Francis   Why Child, I think God called me, and I heard. He planted in my soul such flaming love for him and for all his creatures moving here within the circle of the blessed sun. I must love, too, or die of cold alone. So I have praised the sun and the moon and the stars, the trees, the waters, the great winds that blow. Fire, and sleep and very death herself. And these dear children, too, they are my care. And all the birds that fly in boundless space. Fishes in the sea, the humming bee, even the snake that creeps on the ground. I care for all.

(*Pan creeps in to listen and gradually comes near.*)

Child   Pan! Oh, come closer, you don't need to be afraid.

Francis   I have known Pan since time began. In truth, he is my brother, too. Like me, he loves these helpless things. For him the rose is red, the bees make music, and the wild birds hush themselves to silence, should Pan play his pipes or Francis preach. Brother, kneel here and I who have nothing to give, will bless my brother like this.

(*lays his hand on Pan's head.*)

Francis and Pan will shield these helpless things. And tell all men that they too play their part in the great scheme of things. And none deny their right to man's protection and his love. Come little brothers, come. Here we will sleep on the warm earth until daylight comes.

(*Group of all asleep on the ground.*)

Episode Five

Mars and St. George

Mars stands in the center of the stage alone. He has full classic armor and a large shield.

Mars   Who would believe that I am Mars, that god of old, at whose advance the earth would shake and the red star Aldebaran would blaze in heaven above when Mars went forth to war. Men called me the Avenger, when I drove my chariot. Fright and terror were my steeds of rage that encompassed the whole earth.

Even the sea and sky were afraid when Mars conquered all and rode the path to victory. In Rome, they put up great temples to my name, and worshipped me. Why shouldn't they? Was I not father of their first king, and didn't I guard the sacred city with my shield and sword? Now, what a sad and miserable thing am I! Rome has no need of me, she has fallen on evil days. Her children are cowardly fools to whom the light of battle brings no joy to the shout when Mars goes forth to war. The god must hide his glorious piteous head behind his shield so that no man may declare the hour to strike has come. Better than that it were that Mars should die and make an end. I draw my sword—and ask a Roman's death.

Child   (*entering—and seizing the sword*)

> What are you doing with that sword? How bright it is, how sharp! Didn't you once fight in a great battle with this lovely blade?

Mars   Child, don't you know the sword of Mars—the god of war? I would now fall upon that same steel and make an end—for I see well, men need me not—nor do they need my shining sword.

Child   And you are Mars, and I remember once my mother said the little cupid boy called you his father. Oh, for his sweet sake, you must not die.

Mars   Alas, alas, Cupid is dead also. Men have forgotten love and war. It is so, alas. Give me the sword.

Child   (*clinging*) No, no, you shall not die! Will no one help me, so that the great Mars may not die?

(*Enter St. George*)

George (*taking the sword*)   A sword, with such a blade I fought and killed the mighty dragon, and cast him out. And I freed the world of terror and of death. St. George is my name. Brother, what are you doing here? For brother you are, as all that do bear arms in holy war. What are you doing with your sword?

Mars   Those who have no cause to live, make an end to life.

George   No cause to live? While evil stalks abroad? When wrong, oppression, greed, and more still rule the land? I know you now, the god of fierce battles. You taught my arms to war, my hands to fight. Brother, men call me England's saint, as once they named you patron of mighty Rome. And Trojans called on you in direct need to save the city that they loved so well. On many a battlefield in many a land, the cry has been heard, "For England and St. George!" Beneath the blood-red cross, brother, we too each knowing each, fought manfully and well. In memory therefore, I give the sign and place it on the shield, the red cross burns in token of the flame we lit that set the world ablaze. Brothers in arms, a pledge. My hand in yours.

Mars   Brother, it shall be so. I live indeed.

George   For that same flaming sign that now you bear, stands ever as a witness for the Light.

The manuscript we have breaks off at this point. The remainder has not yet been located. —Ed.

PART TWO: POETRY

These poems are somewhat in order, but as Frances Chesterton never intended for us to read them nor collect them, much less that we should care about them, they are often mysteries. Some have dates, as when Frances wrote in pencil on her own copy that the poem had appeared in a certain newspaper on a certain date. But others were written on the back of an old envelope, a slip of Overroads stationery, or a sheet torn from a notebook. They are often written in soft pencil and difficult to read, especially the ones which are photocopies. And yet, here we are, reading them.

The poems give us clues as to Frances's personality, her humor, her thoughts and feelings, triumphs and tragedies. These clues help piece together a life of the person most important to Gilbert Keith Chesterton.

Note that Gilbert replied to the "Ballade of Past Days" in "Ballade Of A Stand" which is in Part 2 of the *Collected Works*, Volume Ten: Poetry, pg. 390.

Dorothy Edith Collins, secretary and eventually G. K. Chesterton's literary executrix is addressed as "Dear Dorothy" and "Darling Dorothy," as well as "D.D." and "D.E.C."

Pamela and Gertrude Monica are Frances's nieces, daughters of her sister Ethel and Lucian Oldershaw—G.K. Chesterton's Junior Debate Club friend. Sheila is Frances's grand-niece.

On "Is There Freedom Left in England?": These poems were written together by Frances Chesterton's cousin, Margaret Heaton Arndt and Frances. Margaret lived with the Bloggs for a long while during Frances's girlhood, and they became as close as sisters. Margaret married a German professor named Paul Arndt. Both Margaret and Paul were published authors. G.K. Chesterton illustrated Margaret's book of German Fairy Tales (which you can find if you search under the name "Frau Arndt.") Margaret Arndt wrote the first poem, which appeared in the Daily Chronicle on June 12th, 1915. Frances Chesterton's response to her cousin's poem appeared on the same day in the paper. They must have planned this out and submitted the poems together.

In the summer of 1909, Gilbert and Frances moved out to a small place called Overroads in Beaconsfield. Frances met a neighbor, Mrs. Walpole and her daughter Felicity. Mrs. Walpole would eventually come to serve as occasional secretary to Gilbert. Frances wrote a poem to Felicity. The poem was published in *A Book Of English Verse On Infancy And Childhood*, Macmillan and Co., Limited; London, 1921.

"Alle Vogel Sind Schon Da" was published in *Untune the Sky: Poems of Music and the Dance*, compiled by Helen Plotz, Thomas Crowell Company: New York 1957, with permission from A.P. Watt & Son and Miss D. E. Collins, which was taken from the original. The original was published in *The Best Poems of 1935* published by Thomas Moult. It should be noted that Frances was fluent in German as well as French.

"The Small Dreams" was published in the *Ashburton Guardian*, Volume 33, Issue 8519, March 1913, page 3. It also appeared in the *Westminster Gazette*. It was reprinted in *The Living Age*, March 29, 1913, No, 3586, Boston.

"Things to Think About" was published in *The Guardian* (UK) November 27, 1938, just before Frances died.

A BALLADE OF PAST DAYS
TO GKC
(ca.1900)

O where is the fearful wild hair
That once I used to abhor,
And the socks that were not a pair
That I without ceasing went for,
And the paper in pieces you tore
They have gone to the shadowy land
And will never return any more.
    You know I have made my stand.

That remarkable coat and rare
My soul rejected of yore,
The hat you once used to wear,
The boots you held in such store,
They have been and are not: no more
Can you hold them fast in your hand;
Their departure I let you deplore.
    You know I have made my stand.

Where the shirt that made people stare,
Where the button I asked to restore,
Where the hateful expression "Don't care!",
Where the tone I used to implore
    You never to mention the war
Where the chalks, the matches, the sand
You ceaselessly dropped on the floor?
    Gone, for I've made my stand.

Envoy
They have gone to the limitless shore
In the manner in which I had planned;
They will never return any more.
    You know I have made my stand.

FLORENCE, ITALY

MARCH 1900 or 1901

(Signed F.B.—prior to marriage--Ed.)

I wandered away in the dark of the night

Through the woods to the mountains above

And in the first mist of grey early dawn

I found the white city of Love.

See, I return with my treasure and spoils

Overloaded and burdened am I

Come dear folk all, why what will you have

Here are my treasures, come buy.

Here rainbow shifts to keep out the cold

Yet hold fast the warmth of the sun

Such fairy robes, come here take your choice

I've more than enough for each one.

See these rare gems that I wear round my neck

And the flowers I've wreathed in my hair

Grew wild in the streets of the city of Love

I gathered them everywhere.

But one little treasure I guard as my own

My secret. A bright angel said

That men call it death, but he named it Life

My star burning mystically red.

And I who had found the white city of Love

Who so early had wandered afar

The treasure is mine that I have on my breast

Death's red and mystical star.

A CHORD of COLORS

Also called "Sunset in October"

(For GKC, 1900)

The great sky stretches far to East and West

To North and South, all coloured in strange hue

Red, purple, blue and wondrous flaming gold

Colours I vow, known but to me and you.

For see the royal colours proudly flung

The imperial purple, now as for all time

Of Love's great dignity and boundless power

The unchanging seal, the universal sign.

And here is gold, dear heart and oh what gold!

Love's gold that alters all the leaden grey

As once for me, do you remember dear?

You changed grey mourning into golden day.

And what of red, what do we know of red?

Who never saw such red until to-day

Love's red that dyes the mountains and the lake

As my face crimsons when a word you say.

And blue that undisturbèd calm deep blue.

That changes not for sun or storm or tide.

This is the hope that Love for ever keeps

Through life and to the unknown other side.

And here one little cloud so purely white

Soft as a kiss, sweeter than day's first breath.

This the white soul of one we both held dear

The soul of one who chose the lesser death.

ALL SAINTS DAY—WESTMINSTER ABBEY
(pre 1901)

All quiet and still within the great dim church

But for the echoing sound of many feet

Feet of the living breathing human souls

Hushed near to silence in this grey retreat.

Living and dead today strangely one

The dead souls live, today the live souls die.

Here Life and Death have met and understood

Death tells her secret and Life smiles reply.

Here grief has built the soul a spacious house

Where we may breathe an ampler purer air

Here is the sunshine, here the noontide's warmth

Here the birds sing, and morning skies are fair.

So hear the well-loved dead that we can call

Across this shining stretch of pavement stone

The mark is on their foreheads and we know

The sign by which our God has sealed his own.

For we have sealed them with the self-same seal

The seal of death closed fast 'gainst time and shock

Life holds the golden key that breaks the bond

And now and then we turn it in the lock.

We are alive, and these the dead are ours

Sealed on the forehead with God's finger sign

Triumphal death, that maketh dry bones live

Knows naught of tears. So these are mine and thine.

ISLAND DREAMS

(Partial Poem)

Of Island Dreams of palm and coral reef and spice

Of mountain wastes of snow fields and green hills of ice.

To sun and moon, day and night we loved the sea the best

That wraps our England guarding her

  by north and south and west

By east coast too, the waves are rocking her to sleep

And waking up the children though many a one must weep.

For the sea has called for ever to English sons to die

And find their graves in heaving waves

That we at peace may lie...

Underneath the golden sun how we just adored

Rushing where the blue waves break by the long sea board

How the children called and shouted, how we answered too

Wind and wave together, when all the world seemed new.

How the sea foam tossed and tumbled how the sea gulls cried

Dipping grey heads in the water, strong winged in their pride.

Underneath the silver moon how we loved to roam

And watch the great sea rollers breaking into foam

When all was hushed to silence save the noisy sea

And that turned to a murmur whispering tenderly.

TO GERTRUDE MONICA

Sweetheart, I have no wish to know what life

May hold for you of trouble or of joy

You stand there ready with such eager hands

Small hands so strong to make or to destroy.

But I dare pray that you may have and hold

Such things as Eve in blessed Eden knew,

The rush of wings, the call of little lambs,

And woods that hold a secret spark of blue.

May you have eyes to see and ears to hear

The answering throb for scent and sound and sight

Your days be filled with splendour of the sun

More splendid still the spaces of the night.

May your dear feet tread little garden paths

May your dear hands bend down and have their fill

Of violets, whose troubled sweetness sets

The frozen pulse of winter all athrill.

And oh, I pray that you may never miss

The changing face of wind among the corn

And hear the swallow in the reeds and see

The silver gull that tracks the plough at morn.

And may you touch the hands of happy folk

Who laugh and sing beneath the open sky

But may you be alone—ah, quite alone

When you draw near the heart of mystery.

A BALLADE OF AN OPPRESSED WOMAN

(date unknown)

Well here you are! Do take this comfy chair.

You like the fire? Do you take sugar? No?

At last the Woman's Movement's in the air,

We must be strenuous now and strike a blow.

Where did you get that ravishing green bow?

Your sister never answered things I wrote.

My children went to see the Lord Mayor's Show.

I'm sure that women ought to have the vote.

I think that the police were most unfair.

Why does that woman spoil her figure so?

That bit of Chelsea is extremely rare.

The higher woman must evolve and grow.

Women have so much—never mind my toe!

I wish that I could brush my husband's coat.

When will the Beauchamp-Montmorencies go?

    I'm sure that women ought to have the vote.

They say the working woman does not care,

But the poor things of course have sunk so low.

Good heavens! Lady Margaret's dyed her hair.

And evolution proves— (That clock is slow!)

Lord Belper's speaking left me in a glow,

I almost felt inclined to make a note.

There's Mr. Thompson with his wife in tow.

    I'm sure that women ought to have the vote.

L'Envoi

Princess, those men are talking still below,

They'll never come if they begin to quote.

Politics are so tiresome, don't you know.

I'm sure that women ought to have the vote.

THE SMALL DREAMS

(1913)

When I was a young girl I dreamed great dreams

Of giant castles fashioned* on a hill of gold;

The gold is but a gorse-bush, and haply it seems

My castle's but a cottage, now that I am old.

Now that I am old, I dream small dreams

Of tiny feet that falter, and tiny songs unsung,

Though I heard the trumpet blare and saw** red gleams

From the flying feet of Cherubim, when I was young.

When I was a young girl I dreamed long dreams,
Of ever flowing rivers and earth and sky unrolled;
My sky's a window square, the rivers are but streams,
And the earth is a hedged meadow, now that I am old.

Now that I am old, I dream short dreams
Of small warm woods and little paths among;
I who saw stretched shadows and the sun's long beams
On the cedar trees of Lebanon, when I was young.

And youth is a memory with its long deep dreams,
Its venture unadventured, the glory still untold;
But I can*** keep forever, unashamed it seems,
The small dear dreams of comfort, now that I am old.

*Another version has "founded" instead of "fashioned."

**Another version has "caught" rather than "saw."

***Another version has "may" rather than "can."

"Is There Freedom Left in England?"

Daily Chronicle on June 12th, 1915

The Question

(by an Englishwoman in Germany)

Margaret [Heaton] Arndt

Are there bluebells still in England?

    Is there left a happy place

Where they grow in all their glory,

    Nodding with a careless grace?

Are there hedgerows still in England?

    All untrimmed and growing wild,

Honeysuckle and dog-roses,

    Dear to every English child?

Is there joy left in old England?

    Or have children grown so stern,

Thinking only of their duty

And the lessons they must learn.

Is there freedom left in England?

Is my England England still?

Not to be coerced or driven,

Save by choice and of her will?

Oh my country! oh my country!

How I tremble, how I fear

When I see the awful bondage

That has fallen on us here.

May God spare you, oh, my country!

Stamped upon you is the worth

Of a nobler far dominion

Than of force upon the earth.

Forge no chains for children's children;

Still let thy law be liberty.

England, mother country, girded

> By the broad zone of the sea.

The Answer

(by an Englishwoman in her own country)

Frances Chesterton

In deep woods of green England

There are bluebells of such blue

That your heart might stop its beating

Could I send one bloom for greeting

> From our belovèd land

> One bloom for you.

In the hedgerow of your England

The dog-rose softly lies,

And the honeysuckle creeping

Would move you in your weeping

To lift a heavy hand

To dry your eyes.

The children in our England

Are laughing in the lane;

They have heard the cuckoo calling

And summer raindrops falling

Great hopes we planned,

Dear, some remain.

High freedom lives in England,

Though we dreamed that she was dead;

We found her in the fighting,

Mid the shouting and the smiting,

That you in alien land

May lift your head.

England, our holy England,

Dear Mother of me and mine,

Still for liberty is pleading,

Though her very heart is bleeding

      And running in the sand,

      Blood spilt like wine.

Yet she is gay our England,

Her back no sorrows bend,

Her warm arms ever folding,

Her children in their holding,

      Erect and firm to stand,

      Abides the end.

HURT NOT HIS EARTH—ALL SAINTS DAY

(Daily Chronicle, November 2nd, 1917)

High on St. Michael's Hill his angel stands

With sheathèd sword and heavy folded wing

Until insistent comes the word upon the breeze

"Hurt not my earth, my sea, my tender trees

        Nor any living thing.

"Till I have sealed my Saints," Merciful God

Thy sea, thy trees, the earth, thy diadem

Lie broken, darkened, blasted and betrayed

And these thy Saints—who did it unafraid

        Shall no man number them?

Lo! They went forth and crushed thy blossoming earth

And stained with blood the splendour of thy sea

And took thy little trees and made them guns

For their just cause—to fight the evil ones

        Who had made mock of Thee.

What should they do but blacken all thy earth

That men may keep white souls to worship thee?

What should they do but take thy holy tree

That made thy cross and crown of agony

        This their Gethsemane.

And some lie dead upon this bare hill side

And some are quiet beneath the troubled sea

And happier some under this flickering shade

Of a tall poplar tree—lie whole—debt paid

        Of ill, done Lord for Thee.

Four angels know this place where now they sleep

Numbered Saints—who in Thy highway trod

The sign is on their foreheads, where they lie

Thy cross burns red, and Heaven itself shall cry

        "Sealed of the living God."

"He was buried in a little wood, just behind our lines"

        Extract from a soldier's letter.

1.

I know a little wood lies privy to my dreams

But in my waking hours I may not walk its ways,

So secret are its spaces and so hushed it seems

No leaf can stir, nor bird herald the days

    With note of praise.

2.

I know not if my wood of dreams be green or grey

It holds no light nor warmth drawn from God's holy sun

No children leave their flowers neglected in its way,

No woodman's craft is done, or left undone;

    No song is sung.

3.

And all the enfolding night, I search in that strange wood

Thwarted, disconsolate, for one green mound afire

All treasure that I store, and all my hope of good

For one green mound, that holds my heart's desire

    My world entire.

4.

And I am ever mocked, and never find the place

Where low he lies, that once was loved; so desolate,

Lost in the wanderings of that colourless grey space

Of evil wood, that doth intimidate

      With note of fate.

5.

But in my waking hours, I know another wood

Alive from end to end with leaping sun and shade,

Star set with blue-bells where the timid ringdoves brood

And small flies hang on every glancing blade,

      All unafraid.

6.

And there all day the cuckoo calls and the soft rain

Falls patteringly on leaves that hold such wealth of green,

The larch buds are aflame, and where the moss has lain

The shining asphodel is surely seen

      Paramount queen.

7.

And in earth's lovely wood, with beating pulse of life

I walk my easy ways, until the spot be found

Sheltered and summer warm, so near the sounds of strife,

Altar of heart's desire, one dear green mound

One little mound.

A BALLADE of DIFFICULTIES

(circa 1920s)

I find it very hard to get a rest,

I find it harder still to make ends meet,

I often feel emotionally depressed

Because I see my butcher in the street,

And, though I don't believe he means to cheat,

The matter is too serious for a jest.

He charged me ten pence for a pound of meat.

Life is a trying business at the best.

I'm envious of the way my neighbour's dressed,

I hate the cold and long for summer heat,

I try to keep my silly temper lest

My hair should turn out anything but neat.

I summon up a sickly smile to greet

A friend who enters obviously distressed,

And this I find is not an easy feat.

    Life is a trying business at the best.

I would set out upon that joyous quest

To find where peace dwells in her sure retreat

Where I may enter as a welcomed guest,

The feast prepared for me to drink and eat—

Where from the far-off field come very sweet

Low murmurs from the Kingdom of the Blest,

Yet my dull heart will worriedly repeat:

    Life is a trying business at the best.

Envoy

Prince, it may rain or hail or snow or sleet,

But keep this sentence safely in your breast,

It is a maxim very hard to beat;

Life is a trying business at the best.

IN THE MIDDLE WEST
Lines written in dejection near Chicago
(1921)

Along the unhedged, unhuman plains
The furrows stretch in ordered line,
Ocean to ocean roll the trains
Past little groups of oak or pine.
And in the bared and timbered towns
Men live and struggle, laugh and die,
Frontierless, far from flags and crowns
Beneath no banner but the sky.

Deep hid in England's lovely heart
A cross is traced among the trees.
The rumble of the woodman's cart
Rolls with pre-Roman memories,
And little gardens stand ablaze
With our unstalled and startling Spring.
Exiled, I walk familiar ways,
And since I cannot see, I sing.

SHEILA'S SOCKS

I made these socks for Sheila

But I feel bound to say

That as she is a generous child

She may give them away.

Perhaps the Sleeping Beauty

Would fancy sleeping socks

Or perhaps she would present them

To naughty Goldilocks.

And lovely Cinderella

When washing up the crocks

Might like to think she had them

To wear with Sunday frock.

Perhaps your dear Red Riding Hood

As at Grannie's door she knocks

Remember of a sudden

To pull up both her socks.

No they're not for Cinderella

Nor for Red Riding Hood

Beauty must sleep without them

Deep in the rose-fenced wood.

And Goldilocks will run away

To where the Three Bears dwell

Without her hat, without her shoes

Without her socks as well.

For these are socks for Sheila

Which Auntie Dear has made

If Sheila sends her back a kiss

She will be richly paid.

For every stitch's a kiss dear

Of that there is no doubt

For if the socks all fall to bits

Why 'tis love that won't wear out.

TO FELICITY WHO CALLS ME MARY

(as published in *A Book of English Verse, 1921*)

When I was but a tiny child, they chose for me a saint,

Fulfilled of Christian charity and heavenly restraint;

But you have called me Mary, and oh! I joy to hear

The name of God's own Mother come so gaily on the air.

What though my arms be empty, and hers forever press

The Eternal Child who touches you with such divine caress.

Here's another love, Felicity, and oh, sweetheart, drink deep.

That you may laugh more easily, and I forget to weep.

For you have called me Mary, making bitter waters sweet.

TO FELICITY WHO CALLS ME MARY II

(As found in Frances Chesterton's papers, with two additional verses—Ed.)

You go singing through my garden on little dancing feet.

Crying 'Mary, Mary, Mary' with laughter shrill and sweet;

And the lily bud grows paler and the passion flower flames,

As light upon the wandering breeze you toss the name of names.

When I was but a tiny child, they chose for me a saint,

Fulfilled of Christian charity and heavenly restraint;

But you have called me Mary, and oh! I joy to hear

The name of God's own Mother come so gaily on the air.

What though my arms be empty, and hers for ever press

The Eternal Child who touches you with such divine caress.

Here's another love, Felicity, and oh, sweetheart, drink deep.

That you may laugh more easily, and I forget to weep.

For you have called me Mary, making bitter waters sweet.

Oh little soul of happiness, oh little dancing feet;

And I grow bold in honour, that all my spirit shames,

As light upon the wandering breeze you toss the name of names.

AFTER THIS OUR EXILE

Is there a sound, a sound as sweet

As singing lark upon the wing?

A child's glad call across the field?

Or that clear note upon the string

Of harp or breathing violin

That holds a joy but half revealed?

I heard the voice of one held dear,

"Yes there are finer things to hear."

"There is the song the angels sing

High in the starry fields of night

That floats to earth from Godhead where

From depth to depth, from height to height,

A rushing sound in endless flight

Of heavenly wings in ambient air

Fills earth and sky from far and near,

A song that only Shepherds hear."

And is there any scent so rare

As that that pours from out the rose?

Or turnèd earth, the ploughman broke

When gay with life the west-wind blows?

Or perfumed that the high priest knows

The swinging censer's climbing smoke?

"A breath of heaven," I heard him say,

"Lives in a truss of new mown hay."

What taste can with this wine compare

This grape that grew in sun and rain

And glowing gold and red invite

To feast and pledge our love again?

This honey of the hill and plain

This good of sweetness and of light?

"Draw close," he said, "and look upon

This smile a mother gives Her Son."

Can there be anything more soft

Than this bird's feathered downy breast?

Or this small head, that holds the sun

Against my knee so lightly pressed?

Or lover's kiss that seeks the quest

Of all to do, and all undone?

He turned and said "you never knew

How feels Our Lady's robe of blue."

Oh lovely is the sunlit Earth

This golden flower, this blossoming tree

This dancing child, this flying bird

Resplendent, matchless, brave and free!

Or this dear house you built for me.

And something rustled, something stirred,

He looked, and whispered very low

"But I have lovelier things to show."

A little stable, poor and mean

Godhead, enthronèd in the hay

An angel choir, and Star o'erhead

Shepherds and Kings upon their way

The bells ring out "Tis day, tis day

Come you and kneel beside his bed."

Here is our home, he said to me

This is the place, where we would be.

ALL SAINTS DAY

Grey are our souls in the grey of the morning

    Dead souls may be, we who pray for the dead,

Fruitless and chill in the chill of the dawning

Come seeking His comfort of wine and of bread.

Joyous His Saints in the gate of His palace

    Holding His gift full measure pressed o'er;

Heaped on His Paten, deep-filling His Chalice,

    Life more abundant, the wealth of His poor.

His poor, whom He loved and whom we have slighted

    Stand splendid, creative, His glory in sum

And we are the stricken we start back affrighted

    Faint at the vision of His Kingdom come.

His kingdom come with His dead for a token

    The dead souls alive and the living souls dead;

Red lips touch the cup, red lips that have spoken

    Warm hands beloved share His mystical Bread.

Live hands touch live hands in the gold of the morning

    Warm lips yield to lips with no earthen constraints,

Communion of living and dead in the dawning

Right dear in His sight is the death of His Saints.

ALL SAINTS DAY II

No terror can touch them

Whom God has delivered

From evil, from sorrows from the burdens and strife

The crown is untarnished

The palm is unwithered

For the Saints to whom death was fulfillment and life.

In the eyes of the foolish

They died: unregarded

The place of their resting, the land of their birth

The gleam of the sword blade

Beauty discarded

A crumbling of ashes, a handful of earth.

Pain cannot reach them

No cry of the dying

Rends the new heaven in full glory revealed.

No torment of malice

No word of [disposing]

The souls of the [just], His servants are sealed.

TO A CHILD BORN on ALL SAINTS DAY

In the uncharted land from which you came

Oh little life, whose breath is of a day,

Knew you those Holy Ones who bore His Name?

Whom none could conquer and whom none could slay?

And did you look with a baby's eyes of blue

See the White Horse upon Jerusalem's sward

And Him that sat thereon Faithful and True

His blood-stained robe and sharp two-edged sword?

And did you hear with little human ear

His trumpet sound for judgment and for war

And God's white armies rank upon rank appear

With noise of many waters from afar?

Did all His Saints throng close about the Throne

And did you with your tiny folded palms

Touch their washed garments or maybe bolder grown

Ran to some martyred mother's waiting arms?

You may have followed with your infant feet

To where the great Apostles dwell in bliss;

If tired you slept upon the golden street

The Virgin Mary waked you with a kiss.

Ah little Saint, not very hard the way

For you who saw the goal before the race

Who chose to enter here on such a day

Trailing your memories of the Holy Place.

ALL SOULS DAY

Of your charity, pray for his soul

    The soul of a sinner

Forget that he once stooped to beg

    The price of a dinner.

Forget when his masters betrayed him

    He cursed and blasphemed;

Remember a chance to live honest

    To what he had dreamed.

Remember he had but his dream

    When he hung down his head:

Forget that when hungry he stole

    Those two loaves of bread.

Forget that he hated the rich

    Who had made him a slave;

Remember he told them the truth

> They never forgave.

Then let him whom High God hath forgiven

> Of *his* charity pray

For the proud who compelled him to bear

> the heat of the day.

Forget they worse clothed him and fed him

> than cattle are fed:

Remember they kneel now for pardon

> Ere pardon be fled.

Forget their contempt and their foresight

> Their treason and doles;

Remember the greatest of sinners

> and pray for their souls.

BETHLEHEM

Hail Bethlehem, our little house of Bread

Where Shepherds watched and Wise Men came to pray

How poor wast Thou, and mean; how couldst thou hold

The splendour and the glory that is thine today.

For men have turned to gold their walls of rock

That sheltered Him from winter's bitter cold

And hung his Manger with such orient silk

As might have served King Solomon of old.

And where Our Lady held a tiny lamp

With shaded hand, to see her sleeping Son

A thousand candles burn a thousand fires

And put to death the cold stars one by one.

And holy incense floats, an amber haze

Veiling the forms of acolyte and priest

Where once St. Joseph ministered and felt

The homely breath of many a humble beast.

And yet the end of all our hearts desire

Is but to kneel before a little Child

A little Child, half buried in warm hay

Who softly stirred and then contented smiled.

What though we may not bring the Magi's gifts

We who are poor, and have but prayers to give

We pray then as the Shepherds prayed of old

That we may look upon the Lord and live.

A CHILD'S CHRISTMAS LITANY

Before our weary heads we lay

Beside Thine own upon the hay,

Our Litany remains to say;

Pray for us, little Jesu.

When daylight fades upon the hill

And ox and ass and sheep are still

And the moon rises slow and chill,

    Pray for us, little Jesu.

When day returns with golden sun

And singing birds, and night is done

And life itself is but begun,

    Pray for us, little Jesu.

When we are tired at work or play,

When we are home or far away,

When our blue skies seem turned to grey,

    Pray for us, little Jesu.

If in our beds we cannot sleep,

If tears will come and we must weep

As ghostly shadows round us creep,

 Pray for us, little Jesu.

Touch us with Thy tiny hand,

Bless Thy children as they stand,

Bring love and laughter, pity, and

 Pray for us, little Jesu.

COMPENSATIONS

On this wide sofa where I lie

I only see the shivering tips

Of dingy trees and the broad sky

In darkened windows show grey strips

Confined dull and narrow:

Comes the impertinent peep and laughing "cheep"

Of a London sparrow.

I hear the footsteps in the street

The trouble and unceasing roar

That rises, falls in rhythmic beat.

Upon my closed substantial door

With such insistent swell

And through the volumed noise, a cool clear voice

"Sweet violets to sell."

Smoke of a thousand chimneys tall

Hangs heavy in the yellow air

And slowly, heavily the pall

Of London fog is everywhere,

Dreaded, full of alarms

And under its cover, the ardent lover

Holds all heaven in his arms.

I dream of love and birds and flowers,

And gates of vaulted skies flung wide,

And rain on leaves in pattering showers,

The high sun glorious in his pride,

And fields of quivering grain.

Yet a London street holds one secure retreat

Where love and flowers and birds remain.

FIVE A.M.

My heart leaps with the sunrise

And then my soul forgets

How certainly the glory dies

With every sun that sets

The Sun Shines for the youthful

It dies out, earth grows cold

A kiss for the beautiful

A sign for those grown old.

I'm humbled by the gladness

Of every bird that sings

I'm humbled by the sadness

Of every bell that rings.

The birds sing to the living

The bell tolls for the dead

A paean of thanksgiving

A dirge for joys now fled.

If joy comes in the morning

And sorrow in the night

Give me to see the dawning

At the first break of light.

That I die not in the silence

In the dark I cannot see [light]

But when day breaks with violence

Because God calls to the night.

TO DOROTHY IN GRATITUDE

1928

Did you dream there was a room in which

Your heart might live?

That I was poor and you were rich

With gifts to give?

Gifts from a countless store to load

An empty shrine,

Flowers of sacrifice that glowed

Like altar wine.

And did you know you had a hand

To touch and heal?

Standing as a saint may stand

At love's appeal.

And did you guess that comfort came

In the dark night?

Because like some sure candle flame

Burned sanctus light.

You did not know these haunting things,

How should you know?

Unconscious love her treasure flings

To earth below.

I took the gifts, I so hard driven

The road I ride,

And saw the little door in heaven

Stand open wide.

For these dear things you are confessed

As one apart,

Whose purpose holds, whose soul is blessed,

Who has my heart.

TO D.E.C.—A DAUGHTER

(1929)

My soul went groping all the past years through

Searching the barren deserts, for a dream,

A mirage, some foreknowledge or a gleam

Of that long-waited day that should bring you.

Ready and warm the chambers of my heart,

Garnished and 'broidered, treasuries in store;

Many had knocked upon the fast-closed door

But only came to question and depart.

Often I entered in that secret shrine

Left there a thought, a vision or a word.

Sometimes I fancied that the silence stirred

Or that you answered to a call of mine.

Where were you hiding, daughter of desire?

In some far convent hidden from the sun.

Was I an Abbess, you perchance a nun

Wedded to charity, as flame to fire?

Was I your mother—sponsor to your vows

That held you captive to my clinging gown

Did we together seek the heavenly crown

That poverty and chastity bestows?

Or am I Naomi, you my daughter Ruth

Wither I travel will you also go?

My people, yours—my God, it may be so

Your vision too of unimagined truth.

No these are dreams, and you are closer still

Than lovely Ruth, or any holy nun

For you have made my very pulses run

With quickened beat, their purpose to fulfill.

And you have brought a long dead hope to birth

That I should hold a daughter by the hand

Like to myself—and I should see her stand

With serious eyes—and answering smiles of mirth.

There is an empty space that must be filled

There is an empty room that needs a guest

Enter my daughter here you shall find rest

All is for you, for so your mother willed.

MARIA IMMACULATA

A Sonnet to D.E.C. (1930?)

D o you remember how we walked the streets
O f Rome and saw the Queen of Heaven high,
R aised and superb upon Her throne, and threw
O ur roses to Her as we passed Her by?
T he swinging bells rang out the Angelus,
H er head a glory with its starry crown.
Y ou knew She stood for us and all the world,

C hrist's kingdom regnant in the sacred town.
O f all my visions let this never fade,
L ady of Stars, the new moon at your feet,
L et us beloved find Her once again
I n Her bright setting in the dusty street,
N earer and holier to us whose souls have met
S o that you too remember, and I may not forget.

TO DOROTHY: SONNET (1930?)

Why did you call, Beloved, in the night?
And I so near. The merest lift of breath
Had brought me to your arms. What sense of fright,
What sudden knowledge, what presage of death

Made all my world stand empty, ah a cry
That cut the shadows as a hurtling knife
Flies from some tangled ditch where murderers lie
All keen to snap the little cord of life.

Had you aghast seen evil unashamed,
Naked and cruel—or some poor piteous ghost
Caught with cold hands your breast,
or Hell's mouth flamed
An instant—[swish]—the heavy shadow past.

TRINITY OF WITNESS

To D.D.
(Lyme Regis, August 1930)

You left me and the sky turned grey.
"God send the sun," I aching said.
"So cold am I, so drained, so dumb,
I feel alone—abandoned."

Much have I had, yet cry for more,
For warmth, for colour, sun and star,
The tilted moon, the sighing sea,
And all the lovely things that are.

What has she left me of herself,

Her touch, her voice, her serious eyes?
These are not here—yet there are hints
That she was with me—Why here lies

A fold of blue. Full many a time
Wrapped in that blue, I saw her stand
Eager, alert to comfort me.
I feel the healing of her hand,

The human warmth, the human joy,
The living form, the body's line
Here fill the soft and homely gown
She left me as a tangent sign.

This picture too in pride of place
That so enchants her ardent mind,
Is it not fair? This beauty clear
Something of her that stays behind?

That thinking, questing critic self,
Instinct of knowledge and desire,
Uplifted head to catch the wind,
Outstretched hand to reach the fire.

And this, oh this—divinest Saint,
This virgin martyr! Once in Rome
We saw her as asleep she lay
All lovely in the catacomb.

Do you remember? Where she rests
Cecilia of the lyre and palm,
Untouched by death, for ever hears
The chant of credo and of psalm.

Enshrined in marble is your soul,
She bides with me. My pulses beat,
She will not stir, but I shall hear
The coming of familiar feet.

God send the sun and send the day
When we shall find the appointed place
And spirit, body, mind at one,
When I shall greet you, face to face.

ON the VIGIL of ALL SAINTS
to D.E.C.
October 31st, 1932

I wondered as you sought the way
To your inheritance in God
May be the path the saints have trod
Might prove too large a price to pay.

How will she stoop beneath the door
That guards the knowledge from her eyes,
How see the golden shaft that lies
Across the sanctuary floor.

The door so small, the world so wide
New heaven, new earth for mind to roam
Yes in a tiny compass—home
For the wanderer, sanctified.

Firm are the feet that scale the Rock
Proud is the head that humbly bows
Before the Godhead in His House
Holy the hands insistent knock.

As He has turned your heart's gold key
So you impatient at His Door
Have asked for Entrance: never more
to that door closed: bend but the knee.

Lift up the latch, throw wide the gate
Ten thousand saints at break of day
Welcome a pilgrim on the way
That had no further strength to wait.

TECUM

("With You")

(to D.E.C.)

Sometimes my soul is sick for alien skies,

Skies that you know also, and knowing hold

In strong remembrance of our wanderings there,

When English skies are overcast and cold.

The velvet sky—star dinted over Rome

Our Lady's Mantle flung o'er dome and tower

Those lifted witnesses to everlasting truth

Rooted in earth—the challenge tree of power.

That spire, crowned with a cross and queen may wear

Tapering, a flame in buoyant sunset gold

Where Cracow whispers of a nation's faith

Young as her freedom—as her Eagles old.

Oh where the chimes rang to a silver sky

From the flat land of Flanders, looming huge

The old high belfry set in a gold square

Rings in her depths the singing notes of Bruges.

Tho' Paris greeted us with starry tears

She could not hide her rainbow; we saw

The Sainte Chapelle, hoarding refracted light

Spill her crown jewels on tessellated floor.

I see again in California sky

How great Orion rode the vault of night

And there aloft in your secluded tower

Your lamp shown out, one strong clear beam of light.

And there are other skies unvisited

Where we shall stand in sunshine or in rain

And cross perchance the Alcantara Bridge

That reaches to the secret heart of Spain.

We have seen all these things and have been glad

Together; I have sorrowed too; we roam

As weary exiles, prisoners in space

Heeding that roof of cloud that is our home.

Out of your window, here in England's sky

Grey, holding, hiding as her mystery rare

Full rain or snow, high wind or sudden sun,

To fill our hearts with rapture or despair.

Here must we all in ultimate content

Return, as storm-worn Eagle to the nest

Each to his appointed place, at the world's end

The unimagined goal of every quest.

Stay here with me, dear heart, till forth we fare

From grey to gold, and back from gold to grey.

Our pilgrimage goes on—we find our home

Who by God's mercy have not lost the way.

THEREFORE I BLESS THEE O CREATURE of WATER

(1932)

Who made thee flow from fields of Paradise

And with four rivers water all the Earth?

Who changed thy bitterness in scorching sand

Into that sweetness that dissolves the dearth?

Who drove thee springing from the granite rock

And as a fountain filled the desert hole?

Or Who in Cana changed thee into wine

To slake the thirst of Man's immortal soul?

In Jordan's stream who bade the leper wash

Over whose Holy Head was water poured?

Who walked the waves of Galilean lake

On that dark night when Peter knew his Lord?

Who bade thee gush from out His wounded side

That water so may cleanse the stain of blood

The Holiest has shed—and Man restored

To his high place by the baptismal flood?

He, who in chaos parted from dry land

The waters of the impenetrable deep

And over all His Holy Spirit moved

Calling to life from death—to wake from sleep.

Bless Thou Thy creature Water—innocent,

Holy, free from all evil and let him

Become a living fount, a purifying stream

Beneath the wingèd feet of Cherubim.

TO PAMELA, AGED 5

(May 11, 1933)

When I was going to be five

My Mother said, "Now look alive

You're old enough to sweep the floor

Or rub the handles of the door.

And dust the banisters and stairs

And shake the cushions in the chairs,

I'll even let you wheel the pram

And spread the bread with strawberry jam.

And you can ornament the cake

That I have been at pains to make;

This cake must have its candles five,

So Pamela must look alive.

All prepared for birthday tea

For Pam, for Juliet and for me;

A piece for Daddy there's to spare

If he can't promise to be here.

You must be very quiet and good

And only eat the simplest food;

You must not spend the day in bed

But have a lovely time instead.

For only once in all the years

The magic number *five* appears,

The date that ends your baby ways

And leads you into childhood's days.

May you have love and joy and friends

To guide you to the world's far ends;

May you be ever keen, alive

As on the day when you were five.

Pam.

And this is how I felt you see

When thus my Mother spoke to me.

[BERNADETTE]

(Partial poem)

A rushing river and a little town

Mountains of rock flung all across the sky

A peasant girl who lonely treads the field

And listens as the birds go swinging by.

The Queen of Heaven knew that flowering […]

The birds that sang, the river's constant fret

The rocks were hers, the little town,

That field, the flaming soul of Bernadette.

She stood upon the rock beneath the stars

And spoke as never woman spoke before

She who kept all things hidden in her heart

Called on a peasant maid to ope the door.

Fling wide the portals of that mighty door

Wide to the World, her arms outstretched to Love…

…A healing of the nations, could they but see

A simple vision in a darkened cave…

[IN THAT DEAR SONS I'D ASK the KINDLY FOLK]

(Partial Poem)

In that dear sons I'd ask the kindly folk

To let us bide for long unending days

So that we part not on our separate ways

As yet one silver cord unloosed, our golden bowl is broke.

The river runs for other lives than ours

The swan may watch some other lovers pass

The pool reflect again as in a glass

Faces unknown to us, framed in the selfsame reeds and flowers.

Yet may they keep deep hid some little trace

Of us who passed, greeted and said farewell

Trees nod remembrance, or the water swell

The swan slow turn, a low cry from the heron high a pace.

There are for us, the vision in one's eyes

Of one small measure of enchanted ground

Which in the garden and the heath we found

That waits for us, untouched, unchanged,

                    a dream that never dies.

FROM CALVARY to BETHLEHEM

(Partial Poem)

I'd walk in half a day

And wonder if those blessèd feet

That trod the narrow tunneled street

Had halted in the way

Where dark and daylight sudden meet.

[HEATHER and GORSE]

(Partial Poem)

Heather and gorse and the wild birds

The sea and the blessèd sun

A wisp of white cloud folded

Like the wimple of a nun.

Gold and purple transcendent

And silence everywhere

Creeping closer to me closer

Through the honey scented air.

Unfathomable stillness

As hush falls at Sanctus bell

Or that half hour's silence

That in heaven befell.

[ODE to a HYDRANGEA]

(Partial Poem)

How splendid is its stately grace

Stands my great hydrangea

A home it has, or dwelling place

A friend, no stranger.

A pledge of friendship that shall last

Through space and time and danger

A lovely thing, to heal the soul

My very dear hydrangea.

[SPRING]

I sing to men on endless plains

Of little hills, where shadows blue

Drop from great clouds where healing rains

Reveal a beauty ever new.

Here sky is brass and earth is dun

I tell the tale of primrose laid

Beneath bright moss where grieving sun

Shows deeper hollows of green shade.

They tell me of their cities wealth

Their acres yield of gorgeous grain

The land that gives to all men health

So that they labour not in vain.

I cannot answer, yet I know

The secret song that I must sing

My daffodils are all a-glow

For England's woods have caught the Spring.

THE HAPPY FIDDLER

(For D.E.C., June 11th, 1933)

What does he play upon those happy strings

That he should smile at beggar's hat and coat

And ragged arm that golden music flings

Out to a toiling world, pure note on note;

What does he play?

The music of ineffable content

Sings from the spirit of the curving bow;

Listen, oh listen, this is how it went,

Molto vivace —andante—adagio;

Thus did he play.

First quick the air, as spring is light and keen

Then slower as the gathering years take toll

Of youth's bright hours, and all its tears unseen

From the worn body, calling forth the soul

As he did play.

The long-drawn music of unfathomable peace

Adagio of the restless heart of man,

Of heavy burdens bringing the surcease

Of length of living, and of death's short span;

Of this he played.

And playing ever smiled, for well he knew

That he poor fiddler from some summer shore

When e're the bow across the strings he drew

Eased the long exile of the homeless poor;

For them he played.

But not for them alone the moment rare.

The great enchantment of that happy smile;

For love he played upon the vibrant air

The world to harmony; yet all the while

For you he played.

TO MY MOTHER

(About 1933—Ed.)

Across the deep abyss of time and space

God flung a cord between your trembling palms;

One end He held immovable in place

The other lowered to your patient arms.

"Five knots to be unloosed," His word rang free,

"Ere the great rope become the scaling bars

That lead the soul released to hang on ME

Hid in the brightness of a million stars."

You fumbled with the knot and darkness came,

"Must I be blind to find my Lord," you cried,

"No sight of sun or flickering candle light

In this dark night; no torch to be my guide."

You found the second knot and loosed the cord;

"Salt has no savour, sweet things no desire,

Wine is but water meagerly outpoured,

Bread is of ashes dead raked from the fire."

How weary are your fingers, set again

Unravelling the third unyielding strand;

"No scent of rose, nor grass, nor evening rain

And odourless the flowers in my hand."

"I cannot answer to the touch of friends,

I cannot feel the wind upon my head,

I do know now where the far window ends;

Insensitive I lie upon my bed."

The fourth knot remains the last to break;

The sense of sound, the music of the spheres,

The human voice, the song the children make,

All to fall silent on your sealèd ears.

"The lovely things God gave me; His dear gifts;

Smell of wet earth, the trumpet dominant,

The taste of grape, sight of a child that lifts

Clear eyes to mine, the lover's kiss intent.

"The whole long story of my pilgrimage

Far far behind in the deep wells of time,

Far far ahead the height I cannot gauge,

Only this rope that fearfully I climb."

"Hand over hand, foot after foot I grasp

The knotless cord, and with a final breath

I fling away the end, and sudden clasp

Thy Hand, that plucks me through the gates of death."

TO the CHILDREN ACROSS the ROAD

The children came on May Day from the home across the road

The house that stood so empty all winter days and nights

And now there are so many, they have really overflowed

And come to call upon me between the shifting lights.

The youth of all the ageing world comes with each changing May

The May Queen crowned with daisies holds her perpetual court

The king is decked in beech leaves for glory of the day

And Robin Hood so bold of yore, has lived again and fought.

Maid Marian pulls forget-me-nots as blue as are her eyes

All earth is green and golden with promise of the year.

The sturdy tulips amorous blush in sudden sweet surprise

And the swallow wheels untiring in the honey-scented air.

We too have had our May Days when all the world was young

But now the spring is yours and yours the primrose way

We too were kings and queens; but our songs are nearly sung

While God's dear birds are whispering you the secret word of May.

And all things stand eternal; childhood and youth and age.

For us the silver deepens, but you have kept our gold

The gold of all the May Days, yours not for work or wage,

To hold as priceless treasures, when you too shall be old.

LADY DAY

Last night Our Lady whispered to her Son

Lying asleep upon her troubled heart

"I go to find my garden over sea

In that loved isle, set like a jewel apart.

They gave me England for my garden green

England, they said, shall be our Lady's dower

For her the celandine shall lift its head

For her the glory of the sun and shower."

And so last night our Lady came again

To trim the garden we so gladly gave

And in the stillness of the brooding night

She wandered careless with her little Babe.

In deepest woods her robe has touched the moss

And blue the blue-bells of our Lady's gown

The wind flowers white, where her white sleeve has swept

And golden are the cowslips of her crown.

You, that have eyes to see may know she passed

Up the long roads and through the woods asleep

For love of her the fields are gold today

And for her sorrow all the song birds weep.

OUR LADY'S DAY

Our Lady, ours no longer, we have left her and she weeps
For another sorrow added to the burdens that she bore
Another sword to pierce her heart. Oh Queen of all the world

We have rent the robe you came in, and broke the crown you wore.

And Gabriel's lily lies ashamed and crushed beneath our feet
And his white doves of the innocent pledged for unhallowed gold
The Mystic Rose lies bleeding, his Tower of Ivory stained
For woman's cast her out today, whom men cast out of old.

Though we saw the Queen of Heaven circle high above the moon
And set our tapers burning for glory at her feet
Her daughters reap this whirlwind of man's madness and disdain
Who mock with cruel laughter her sisters in the street.

Women defiled her altars, and men may wait in vain
For the love call of the Spring time, the splendor of full years
For motherhood transcendent, the exceeding great reward
For this sorrow hid with smiling, this smiling born of tears.

Oh Mary, Queen of Heaven, come in our bitter need
Ere men shall say of women, they knew not what they did

Mother of God have mercy, open thine arms and pray
That our pride be brought to tatters, and all our shame belied.

ORA PRO NOBIS

(Pray For Us)

To meet Our Lady face to face

Our Lady in so fair a place

Above the moon, beneath sore feet

At little shrines on busy street

Forgotten courts and arches where

The sunlight falls within the square

High walled—spacious

Delicate—gracious.

And all her heart a prayer.

The oil lamps burning dim

In hidden corners…

PRAYER

Grant me this wish, Oh God, I pray

Before the ending of my day.

THERE is a SINGING in my HEART

(Partial Poem)

There is a Singing in my Heart

That answers all the bells of Rome

Bells that toss so [clear] a note

From belfry near or hills remote

On shimmering vault

The loud assault

That storms the very gates of day

And rushing tears the veil away

Turned earth and heaven the empty place

Fortress of sound

Bound on rebound

From tower and church and campanell (*sic*)

The whole of a Roman swinging bell

There is a singing in my heart

That answers all the bells of Rome.

ALMOND TREES

(Partial Poem)

The almond trees are glowing flushed and white

In the last rays of the day's soft light

Swiftly the grey clouds usher in the night.

Miserere.*

The little village welcomes in the dark

With twinkling lights and in the distance, hark

The slow chant as the toiling footsteps mark.

The well worn road abreast of the great hill

The air is vibrant with the sounds that fill

The empty faces, and all else is still.

Miserere.

The slow procession takes the upward way

From the bright church to where the outer grey

Marks with soft tones, the closing of the day.

Above grey walls the gleaming torches shine

Backward and forward on the wavering line

The sad notes fall, as the last rays decline.

    Miserere.

You keep the vigil children of a land

Of sun and sir…

*_"Have mercy."_

[AVILION]

(Partial Poem)

We rode once at eve through the vale of Avilion

Where hedgerows alone are noisy with birds

And there fell on our souls the peace of oblivion

The hurl of harsh voices, the ending of words.

For words had been spoken, though words had no meaning

For words had been cruel, cruel as a blow

But the vale of Avilion left us to dreaming

Where the blossoming thorn is whiter than snow.

POPPIES

(Partial Poem)

Poppies have reared their haunting heads

Thrusting red blooms in pride of place

Splendid and gay a-shimmer as many a maid

with laughing eyes and painted face.

And need their leaves to hide his grief

For Love lies bleeding, hurt to death

As many a lover, wounded sore

At careless feet sighs his last breath.

Untouched by heat the sunflower lifts

His golden petals to the sky

Turning for warmth to burning south

The home of his nativity.

In the deep woods in hedgerow dark

The nightshade hides the flower of doom

What evil thoughts what secret wine

Lies hidden in that orange perfume.

Queen of her Kingdom, loveliest rose

Prodigal beauty flings abroad…

[EVE]

When Eve first opened wide enchanted eyes

In a green garden, this world's Paradise

What caught her wondering fancy as she raised

Her lovely head to cloudless blue or gazed

With questioning glance

At soft advance

Of bird and beast? Creatrix deified.

This first—and last of wonders—Adam's bride

What came she forth to see that primal day

Ere mate or children stole her love away?

The swaying top of some full blossomed tree

Tossing bright petals laughing to be free

Of wind and sunshine—or the shimmering reed

That fringe Euphrates stream, four rivers lead

To golden sands

Of desert lands

The freshness of that earliest tender dawning

The glory of a woman's first adoring

What caught her gaze that unimagined day

Ere sin and death drove innocence away?

On that lone tree in central garden set

Holding its fateful secret, unknown yet

Of God's fore-knowledge—good and ill

And His first gift, man's freedom of the will

Did hiss of snake

Call her awake

Or voice of singing birds assail her ear

And she entranced arose and dreamed to hear

The love song of that earliest bridal day

Ere grief and anger shut all sounds away…

[Epilogue to a Play, found among Frances Chesterton's poetry. This Epilogue doesn't seem to go with the known plays of Frances's.—Ed.]

EPILOGUE

Our tale is told, our play is done

Time calls us, and we must

Leave these old stories of an age

To crumble into dust.

Yet, from the dust this ancient king

In centuries remote

Saw English skies, walked English ways

And heard the blackbird's note.

He saw the tides in Severn fall

He knew the purple hills

The dreaming woods, the level fields

The English ploughman tills.

And they were his—his hills, his woods

His skies and winding road

The river's edge, the fields of corn

The waggoner's full load.

And they are ours—we share with him

Far greater things than these

A Mother in a stable bare

With a Child upon Her knees.

And for that Mother and that Child

His faith and ours we pray

Kneel with him at the manger shrine

on every Christmas Day.

PAX VOBISCUM

(Peace Be With You)

Where are you wandering
Men of good will?
Seeking for peace
Ever seeking her still.

Where is her dwelling place?
In the wide sky?
Question the stars
They make no reply.

In the rush of the wind,
On the sea's bed,
From high mountain top
Peace reluctant has fled.

In the cities of men
A deluge of sound
Where honour is lost
Is peace to be found?

Then where can you find her
Men of good will?
Earth does not hold her
Nor valley, nor hill.

In the heavens bespangled
Countless the stars,
And greater than all
Flames the splendour of Mars.

But somewhere an ass brays
Oxen low soft,
A twitter of birds
On the rafters aloft.

Here a Maiden and Mother
With Child new-born
Bare ruined stable
Storm beaten and worn.

Holes in the patched roof
Peace covers with wings;
Here is her dwelling
'Mid unthinkable things.

And the Angels sing "Glory"
With heavenly mirth
And men of good will
Cry "Peace upon Earth."

THE FEAST of the PURIFICATION, CANDLEMAS

Bright air, strong water and devouring fire,

Three elements ordained by ancient lore

To re-create and purify man's soul;

Inviolate keep their power to restore.

How strained the image that our God conceived:

Fitful the flame that burns in heavy air;

Darkened the waters flowing from the rock

New prophets strike, that no assuagement bear.

How shall we tell of that clear upper air

Where Mary's doves in silver silence wait

And cleanse bright wings, or lower shining heads

For Presentation at the Temple gate?

Can air thus purify the body's ill?

Shall not His wind come sweeping rushing through

The house of life and bid His image stand

As He had willed it who made all things new?

And water flowing from a thousand streams

Dig its deep channels, bearing out to sea

The dust, the slime, earth's doubtful merchandise

Down to the depths of that infinity?

Water, the holy healer of man's sin,

Breaks through the secret lumber of the mind

That harbours all the sophistries of wrong

That makes His creature, deaf and dumb and blind.

Here in this little corner is a taper set

A dim gold flake that flickers and burns low

A blessed light caught from the Holy Place

As from the sun Prometheus long ago—

Stole the great ray, Hephaestus' ancient might,

To warm, deserted so, the heart of man;

So shall this purifying candle's eye

Challenge the fire of flaming Aldebaran.

Blow wind, rush water, holy candles burn!

Wind of our God, renew thy Pentecost;

Baptismal waters, plunge us in the flood;

Save thou thy children that they be not lost.

Give them thy tapers, rise up fire divine,

Consume, convert, unfathomable ray!

Our flaming pillar, visible in night

To burn until the coming of the day.

"ALLE VOGEL SIND SCHON DA"

(All the Birds are Already There)

(Played by a Musical Box)

(1935)

Are all the birds imprisoned there

Caught in that box of tinkling sound?

Birds from some fairy forest where

Their little ghosts move round and round.

Their bright breasts hidden in this cell

That holds the magic of a bird's

First morning song, the lovely swell

Of lifted notes that ask no words.

An air, perhaps, Scarlatti knew,

Or Mozart heard an angel sing,

As some enchanted blackbird flew

To herald an orchestral spring.

This secret life that hides within,

That joyous air, that happy store,

Held captive in this painted tin

For us, who now can sing no more.

LONDON LEAVES

(Westminster Gazette, November 13th no year given—Ed.)

Oh golden leaves of London, dancing in the sun

Don't you know, oh, don't you know that winter has begun

That far north on the uplands is the white breath of frost

And sadly moans the wind there for summer days now lost

And black in lonely fields stand stricken barley sheaves

But bright the sun is dancing on London's golden leaves.

Cold are the furrows where the ploughman goes to plough

And copper red the carpet beneath the beech tree now

By the river's edge the boatman moors a useless boat

And the low cry of the plover comes soft and remote

Grieving for the beauty gone, as a lover grieves,

But bright the sun is dancing on London's golden leaves.

Oh golden leaves of London dancing in the sun

Your day is almost over, your course is well night done

For see o'er chimney pots and towers the drear fog hides

And far away behind the roofs, the low cloud rides

For sure and silent, undeterred, the steps of winter run

And London leaves, alas* no longer, dancing in the sun.

*A second version replaces "alas" with "oh God."

"MAN HAS FOUND NO COMFORT in the GRAVE"

I would not have the long past years return

I want as glad renewal of the spring

I had my youth and treasured it, and now

I have no fear of what dread death may bring.

Fear? but I have my fear, fear I grow cold

To all I knew on this beloved earth

That birds may sing their song for me in vain

That children will not call me in their mirth.

That all that men have thought in lovely rhyme

All the wealth stored that harmony combine

The sighing breeze, God's thunder in the air

May find no echo in this heart of mine.

That man may do great deeds and yet as fire

Burn in my soul to quick responsive word

Oppression stalk abroad and greed encroach

Thy notice nigh and I not draw the sword.

Fear that I ask for peace in these last days

No need to smile and more as need to weep

I who once laughed that I should fighting die

Now like a craven one content with sleep.

Content? Not if one throb of headstrong youth

Cry from the depths of peace for which I crave

With answering shout for glory of man's soul

That will not find his comfort in the grave.

NOVEMBER

(Most likely 1936—Ed.)

I wandered aimless in the dreary grey

Colour was none, not any hint of blue

Solemn and deathly very far away

The bells rang out, dear heart, for you for you

Your dreams so many, and your years so few

Your full years changed to void, your dreams to clay

And I who shared all this endure too

    Cold and alone on this November day.

I knew you silent after all this fray

Your face in quiet death so strange a hue

I stood aside, that I might not betray

What none had dreamed, my love for you, for you

How could we then our secret vows renew

Where other folk may enter here to pray

We may not wed. Death will not let us woo

We part unblessed on this November day.

Part did I say, and yet perchance it may

Prove not a meeting for such lovers true

Parting the price I did agree to pay

Because my love was all for you, for you

Meeting because this sun has broken through

And set on your dead face a golden ray

That we this ancient covenant renew

A smile for me on this November Day.

THE SUMMONS

Little Child Jesus, asleep in the Manger,

Gather the pilgrim, the outcast, the stranger,

Summon the tramp from the pitiless road,

A vagrant, an outlaw of no fixed abode;

    Have mercy on these

    Who now on their knees

No longer are homeless, at the end of the day;

They sleep near Thy bed in the comforting hay,

Deep in that peace no man taketh away.

Call to the great ones who rule the wide spaces,

Summon the tyrants with merciless faces,

Bid them lay at Thy feet, the scepter, the crown,

Their silver, their gold, their greed of renown;

        Have mercy on these

        Who now on their knees

Stripped naked and bare in the cold light of day

Have nothing to offer and nothing can pay,

Who too ask for warmth in the comforting hay.

Oh, Queen of heaven, high enthroned in a stall,

Call to the children, the Innocents all

To see thy fair Son as He sleeps in His bed

With hay for His cover, and straw for His head;

        Love incarnate for these

        Who now on their knees

With bowed heads and hands folded ready to pray,

Kneel by His throne of sweet-scented hay

Till darkness is vanquished and light comes with day.

THE RETURN of the RIVER

(to GKC)

Do you remember how a river runs

Between low banks and how the old white mill

Turns a perpetual wheel when all is still

And in the pool the clear reflection of a thousand suns.

And do you see again the high white cloud

That dropped its shadow on the gleaming grass

The swans superb that turned to watch us pass

And do you hear once more

    the dove proclaim her grief aloud.

How broad the heron spreads her chequered wings

Across low flats, where many an ancient tree

Does its slow death, is filled of memory

Of greatness gone, such thoughts

    as stir the minds of banished kings.

And by the river's edge the untroubled town

That we so loved, when once we wandered there

And found our youth, or something yet more rare

Content of time, robbed for a measured space

    of smile or frown.

I'd give you back those dear and drifting hours

I'd call to bird and bid the river flow

Brimful for us, so that we should but know

Once more the large fulfillment

    of that moment that was ours.

THE UNFORGOTTEN FEET

Mid all the noises of the world I know

The moving sound of dear remembered feet

For very joy and fear I hold my breath

And bid the blood of life more faintly beat.

For oh! They move so lightly o'er the grass,

So careful are the footsteps of the dead

They would not startle by a sudden sound

The tiny wren that whispers overhead.

Oh dear loved feet that walked the ways with me

Along still paths or in the dusty street

There is no sound in all this calling earth

To hide the measured music of your feet.

I know your foot fall 'mid a thousand more

None of God's children, standing in His sun

Walking this earth with sad or happy tread

Can move my soul as this remembered one.

Who wanders in the courts of Paradise,

Or moves in heaven with uplifted head

Yet walks beside me, though none else may hear

So careful are the footsteps of the dead.

In Memory of G.K.C., 14th June, 1936

"Fair Shine the Day on the House with Open Door"

(R.L. Stevenson)

In the sure sanctuary of your spreading roof-tree

Each restless thought was folded into peace

And all my heart's nostalgia would cease,

Assuaged in your great house of charity.

Your hand was stretched to all who knocked: "Hail, friend!"

And which of those who hungered was not fed

With wine of your warm mirth, with wisdom's bread?

The door stood wide; the hearth glowed to the end.

In the third watch when the slow hours tramp

On heavy, heavy feet towards the light,

The last guest entered…every pane was bright,

And the slow, kind hand of death turned out the lamp.

The day is fair…but will your house put off

Its firelit front of hospitality?

Rooted in peace and reared in light, your tree,

And all my prayers rest in the boughs thereof.

The word of welcome may be left unsaid,

Strongest in silence. Shall I find

Your shining morning face less kind

Than when at twilight while the logs burned red—

We shared the sacramental wine and bread?...

The door stands wide, and I am comforted.

THE PRIORY, 1886-1936

"CARITAS"

Faith, Hope, and Charity—these three;

And the greatest of these is Charity:

Your challenge and password,

Your unsheathed sword,

Who keep the fortress of the Lord;

Our solace, our stay in hopes and fears;

Your vision through these fifty years.

C

Children, spirited, grave and gay,

Set in the straight and narrow way,

Fostered in the faith and constancy

To know their laws are liberty,

Who serve the right, the just, the pure;

Minds multiform that life will find

Stamped with the Cross, with courage signed

And the Counsels that endure.

A

Authority, whose wise and moderate rule

Solves problems wider than we meet at school:

Balance, restraint and fealty shall be

Our bulwarks in a world of anarchy;

Asceticism—Heavenly-scaling power—

In its solitary garden grows

Hidden, inviolate, the Mystic Rose,

Dark consolation of the passion-flower.

R

Religion, bearing on its blazoned scroll

The blood-red script of the Martyrs' Roll;

Purple and gold of the Liturgy;

The Chalice; the Keys to bind and free;

The triumphal progress of the King,

When the Cross is raised, the banners fill

In the following breeze and down the hill

The silver censers swing;

When candle-flames, each a lifted blade,

Are dim in the sunlight, bright in the shade,

Through cloister and cemetery they glow

To Sion's strong praise, as the bell rings low

And in field and garden the fertile sod

Is cloaked and hushed by the scented shower

Of marigold, rose and lily-flower

Strewn in the pathway of God.

I

Innocence clothed in the armour of light:

The lamp of our peace burned steady and bright,

Tended through those storm-racked years

When youth and childhood part with tears;

Saga unsung and tale untold

Of those whose patient, daily toil

Drives the first flails through untried soil,

Who labour not for fame, nor gold.

T

Traditions held and loyally served;

As sacred wine the Truth preserved,

Proud legacy of the centuries

In an age of cowardly casuistries;

Its height, its depth, we cannot gauge—

As in a glass we darkly see

Its beauty veiled and dim—but we

Do not forget our heritage.

A

Augustine of the heart of flame,

Our Rule perpetuates his name;

Through tracts of intellectual drought

The crystal fountain of his thought,

Still singing, springs; we understand

That sanctity is wisdom's prize,

When God has touched the poet's eyes

Knowledge and love walk hand-in-hand.

S

Spirit of solitude, wherein is sought

The stillness that lies at the core of thought;

Through the tempest of time our hungering race

Remembers the habit of one far place;

Our scattered selves are anchored there

So we may bear untarnished, whole,

The essential quiet of the soul

Whose silence is its strongest prayer.

Faith, Hope, and Charity—these three;

But the name of Christ is Charity.

The Observer, on Sunday October 3, 1937 on page 30 published a collection of poems and memories dedicated to the demise of the tram service in London. Frances entered G.K. posthumously in the contest with these words modified from *The Club of Queer Trades:*

Perhaps the most perfect place for talking on earth: the top of a totally deserted tramcar. To talk on the top of a hill is superb, but to talk on the top of a flying hill is a fairy tale.

Then Frances herself entered this poem:

> Must we forever say a long farewell
>
> To that most perfect place for lovers' talk;
>
> Deserted tramcar riding through the night;
>
> Our fairy tale is ended—Let us walk.

> No trolley bus shall hold us in its thrall
>
> As that bright ship from Hammersmith to Kew,
>
> Farewell, loved link with my romantic past,
>
> I'd rather walk; farewell, dear tram, to you.

TO A WEEPING WILLOW in CANDLEMAS LANE

A Meditation on Easter Eve

(Easter Eve, 1937)

I saw a golden willow

Weeping in the sun

Why do you weep oh willow

If spring time has come?

Why do your bending branches

Droop down to the ground

When the birds in your shelter

Their love songs have found?

When the soft west wind whispers

Oh! Why do you sigh

When your oriflamme banners

Challenge the sky?

"Oh I weep for the spring day

That never remains

I weep for the dead birds

That winter has slain.

And I mourn with the west wind

That brings bitter tears

For the cry of the Mother

That nobody hears.

For God's dead Son forgotten

And laid in a grave

Nailed to a Cross: and of death

Of the young and the brave.

But I toss my glittering leaves

In a glory of gold

Noble banners of victory

When a stone is rolled.

From the dark sealèd tomb,

He is risen. He said

Death hath no more dominion

For I am not dead.

The souls of the faithful

I hold in My Hand

Though in Adam they died

Here living they stand.

And I, a weeping willow

Laugh in the Sun

For death has been vanquished

And Life has begun."

WHO MOVED THE STONE?

A dark bird flew across an empty sky,

Empty of sun, or moon or cloud,

Filled with the rushing wind of high

Imprisoned spring; he piteously

Calling from death to Life aloud,

"Unloose the bonds, shake off the shroud."

So called the bird to sleeping earth

To empty sky; advancing night

Crushing the very pangs of birth

With iron hands, that none comes forth

To meet the challenge, nor delight

The one dark bird in restless flight.

Ever he wheeled in wind-swept space

Invoking warmth from treacherous cold,

Living from dead, spring from winter's face,

Love from the mourner's sad embrace;

Calling his mate, from field, from fold,

"Unloose the bonds, be bold, be bold."

The two birds circled in the air

With wings a-quivering and bright;

A dark bird, and the second fair,

As single lost—the perfect pair;

Ever together, flight on flight

"The bonds are loose, the shroud is light."

Oh birds of beauty, birds of spring,

Oh tellers of some Easter day

Proclaim aloud, take wing, take wing,

That life so greatly triumphing

Rolled the vast stone of death away

That could not hold that Holy Clay.

THINGS TO THINK ABOUT

(1938)

If I were a poet I would often scatter seeds

As letters of the alphabet sown all along the way,

A would come up <u>A</u>ngel, or maybe <u>A</u>sphodel,

B would be a <u>B</u>ayard brave, and **C** a <u>C</u>hristmas Day.

And **D** might turn to <u>D</u>aphne and **E**, <u>E</u>lysium,

F to pure <u>F</u>elicity and **G** to <u>G</u>entleness.

And **H** the things that <u>H</u>oly are and humble men of heart,

With **I**seult of the healing hand, and **J** for <u>J</u>oyousness.

And then that long lost **K**ingdom, hidden in the deep

The **L**and of **L**yonesse that I shall never see;

And if I were a poet, I should apprehend

The sorrows of the **M**agdalen, the grief of **N**aomi.

And **O** to be my **O**dyssey, my sailing and my end

To find in **P**aradise fulfillment of the **Q**uest;

In **R**oncesvals with **R**oland to hear the holy horn

Blown from the towers of **S**arratt in a vision of the blest.

The **T**roubadours went singing when all the world was young.

Their lutes are silent now beneath the apple foam,

Yet **U**nfinished is the symphony, the music of the spheres,

The tragedy, the comforting, man's prison, and man's home.

And **V** shall stand for **V**enice, of cities paramount

Where **V**enus too might rise again from out a silver sea.

And here is **W**ater changed to **W**ine as once the spoken **W**ord

Went forth at Cana's marriage feast in far-off Galilee.

Xanthos, swift as the wind, the wonder horse of old

And **Y** the Yggdrasil, the tree of endless age,

To where God reigned alone on the mountain height of Zion.

Jerusalem of the golden gates, the end of pilgrimage.

If I were a poet, I would sow these magic seeds

The seeds of lovely words to grow in sun or shade.

But I can only think upon these things and wait

Till God shall tell me how to plant the flowers that never fade.

PART THREE: CHRISTMAS CARD POETRY

Editor's notes on The Chesterton Christmas Card Collection

The Christmas cards are all imprinted with the Chestertons' names, and they list Frances first, interestingly. "With Greetings from Frances and Gilbert Chesterton" is the common phrase of almost all—in 1930 the names were reversed, and in 1937 the card has just Frances's name.

Many thanks to the Marion E. Wade Center in Wheaton, IL for their help with these poems.

The 1917 poem "How Far Is It To Bethlehem" is Frances Chesterton's most famous poem of all her work. An alternate title is "Children's Song of the Nativity". This poem has never been out of print. It was included in the Frances Chesterton original play, *Sir Cleges* in 1924 (see above). It has been included in anthologies, collected in "Best Works" books, and also set to song. The music is a traditional English tune known as "Stowey" in the 16-18th Centuries.

For example, this poem was selected in 1922 in *The Best Poems of 1922* compiled by Thomas Moult. It was collected in *The Magic Carpet: Poems for Travelers* selected by Mrs. Waldo Richards, Houghton Mifflin, 1924. It was in *A Child's Thought of God: Religious Poems for Children* collected by Esther A. Gillespie published in 2006.

"How Far is it to Bethlehem" also appears in Percy Dearmer, et. al., eds., *The Oxford Book of Carols*, Oxford: Oxford University Press, 1928.

"The Crusader's Carol" appears in Frances Chesterton's play *The Children's Crusade* (found earlier in this volume). Published as "The Shepherds Found Thee By Night", Music by Geoffrey Shaw, published by Novello and Company, Ltd., New York, 1923.

"A Lullaby Carol" was set to song, with music by Geoffrey Shaw in 1926.

"Gold, Frankincense and Myrrh" was called "Carol of the Kings" in Frances Chesterton's play *The Three Kings*, found earlier in this volume.

"Lux Mundi" was published in *G.K.'s Weekly*, December 7, 1933 and also on the 1933 Christmas Card.

"In Coelo Et Terra" was published in *G.K.'s Weekly* December 13, 1934 and also on the 1934 Christmas Card.

Christmas 1911

In her warm arms Our Lady holds her Son

That He may see the world beneath His feet,

The little homes where little brothers dwell

Who wake to welcome Him in every street.

And children stir in little tumbled beds,

Turning awed faces to the clouded sky;

They see our little Lord with fluttering hand,

And hear the tread of shepherds trampling by.

The morning breaks with sun and shout and song,

The golden stars grow sudden grey and dim;

We hear the children whisper in the dawn,

He, lifted up, shall draw us all to Him.

Christmas 1912

Upon a little bank of grass

Our Lady and Our Lord.

He dreams of heaven; she of Him;

He hears the wings of Seraphim,

And Gabriel and the Cherubim,

And Michael with his sword.

But while the face of Jesus smiles,

And angels stand a-near,

She hears the curse, the cries of scorn,

She sees the cross, a crown of thorn;

He smiles again, the newly born,

And she forgets her fear.

And Mary looking on Her Son

Doth all His splendour see,

The cross is glory, gold the crown

Love, Honour, Wisdom and renown

Are His, who from high heaven came down

To lie on Mary's knee.

[1913 written by GKC ("Step softly, under snow or rain")—Ed.]

Christmas 1917

HOW FAR IS IT TO BETHLEHEM?

How far is it to Bethlehem?
Not very far.
Shall we find the stable room
Lit by the star?

Can we see the little Child?
Is He within?
If we lift the wooden latch
May we go in?

May we stroke the creatures there
Ox, ass, or sheep?

May we peep like them and see
Jesus asleep?

If we touch His tiny hand
Will He awake?
Will He know we've come so far
Just for His sake?

Great kings have precious gifts
And we have nought;
Little smiles and little tears
Are all we have brought.

For all weary children
Mary must weep,
Here, on His bed of straw
Sleep, children, sleep.

God in His mother's arms
Babes in the byre,
Sleep, as they sleep who find
Their Heart's Desire.

Christmas 1918

SEEN and UNSEEN

The Child lay nestled in the hay,

Sweet scented hay;

Through the gaping door props,

Peeped in the day.

St. Joseph held the tiny hand,

Fast in his own;

"What will life hold for Him

When He is grown?"

"Life holds dread death for Him;"

Our Lady said;

Her loving fingers stroked

The downy head.

St. Joseph kissed the little mouth;

"When He grows old,

Our undying love is His,

Our love untold."

"And the black hate of cruel men;"

His Mother cried;

And folded the woolen wrap

Fallen aside.

St. Joseph warmed the baby feet

Against his breast;

"Millions shall fight and die,

That He may rest."

And Mary hushed the Babe that wept;

"He will give peace,*

He burns the chariots in the fire**

And wars shall cease."***

"How wonderful this mortal Babe,

Here where He lies;"

St. Joseph watched the starry smile

In the sweet eyes.

Our Lady moved across the floor

A tip-toe she trod,

"Hush! that we may not wake

The Son of God."

*Aggeus/Haggai 2:10(9) **Joshua 11:6 ***Psalm 45(46):10

Note: It is probably significant that World War One ended in 1918--Ed.

Christmas 1920

A GERMAN CAROL of the 16th CENTURY

It was very late, and very cold

    at Our Lord's birth

A fig tree stood, the sole green thing

    upon the earth

"Ah Mary harken unto me

    The figs must bide upon the tree

A weary way to go have we

    to find a hearth."

And so when our dear Lady came

    to the open door

"Take us in I pray," said she

    "For we are poor."

        And this my little newborn son

        To him, friend, must us […] be done

        Or you would ere the [willow's] sun

[Repent] you sore.

In truth, with right good will indeed, poor folk

    The good man cried

Safe in any stable

    Tonight may you bide.

But when he heard full […] sound

He hurried o'er the frozen ground

Trembling for fear lest it be found

That they had died.

Arise my wife, dear love arise

A great fire light

The little babe in danger lies

in the cold night.

And joyfully he brought them in

And gave them kindly welcoming

The poor folk followed wondering

Amazèd quite.

Glad to the fire our Lady came

that […] hour

The goodman's roof, the goodman's breath

Our Lady's bower

And Joseph just where he did sit

Set a pot down where fire was lit

And the little snow Christ dropped in it

Turned into flour.

And a little ice he dropped therein

was sugar sweet

The water that he dropped therein

pure milk to heat,

The pot above the fire was hung

Soft was the song that Mary sung,

The little Babe with joy up-sprung

Upon his feet.

Joseph from a block of wood

carvèd a spoon

And ivory and diamond

shone like the moon

And there beneath their wondering eyes

lay little Jesus small and wise

Our Lady feeds him and he lies

In slumber soon.

Christmas 1921

THE BEASTS of BURDEN

The	Great Alexander in triumphal hour
Elephant	Sat his imperial throne
Speaks	Upon my back, and in his moving tower
	He heard the trumpets blown;
	The Conqueror of East and West
	He saw the captives run
	By the veiled sides of his palanquin
	On the road to Babylon.

The   They laid the Holy Carpet on my back

Camel   And bowed down to the dust

Speaks   When Mohamed, the Holy One,

               Fought the battle of the just;

               I strode the desert like a ship

               That sails the pathless sea,

               For Allah's Prophet in his pride

               Was borne aloft by me.

The   When shouting crowds

Horse   acclaimed the Christian King

Speaks   From the Danube to the Rhine,

               My milk-white skin they clothed in gold

               With a red cross for a sign;

               I trod the lowly streets of Rome,

               The plains of Aquitaine,

               And heard great Roland's horn proclaim

               The might of Charlemagne.

The	They gave me nought but bitter blows of
Ass	shame,
Speaks	I, bearer of all men's waste,

There through the Dung Gate they bade me pass

And cursed me in their haste;

But I held my peace as the sharp goad fell,

Nor quivered at the rod,

For I have borne on my battered back

God and the Mother of God.

Christmas 1922

A BALLADE of CHRISTMAS

The moon has shed a sudden light,

The sky has spread a shining way,

Above the inn the star burns bright,

We tread the path before the day;

We, Shepherds poor, we go to pray,

Before a Manger cold and bare,

For cradled in a little hay

The Lord of all the World lies there.

The desert track is dark to-night

The palm trees turn from green to grey,

One Star alone burns in the height

Across the vault one gleaming ray

Falls on a roof: from far away

We, Wise Men with an offering rare,

All eager at His feet to lay,

The Lord of all the World lies there.

And what of us? Shall we have sight

Of that poor bed and shall we stay

To offer gifts for His delight

And like the humble Shepherds pray?

We, too, would lowliest homage pay

To Holy Child and Mother, where

Between split rafters breaks the day

The Lord of all the World lies there.

Envoy.

Prince, Wielder of the Sword of Might

Babe of an hour, so weak and fair,

We, too, would see this holy night

The Lord of all the World lies there.

Christmas 1923

THE CRUSADERS' CAROL

(aka The Shepherds Found Thee by Night)

The Shepherds found Thee by night, by night

Seeing the Star so bright, so bright

Ah me! it was a goodly sight

On Christmas Day in the morning.

Three Kings came from the East, the East,

The great to pray with the least, the least,

Ready to keep the Holy Feast

On Christmas Day in the morning.

The strangest sight they saw, they saw,

A Child on a bed of straw, of straw,

Their souls were filled with holy awe

On Christmas Day in the morning.

You that have come afar, afar,

Soldiers of His in war, in war

Come, oh come, where the true hearts are

On Christmas Day in the morning.

Enter here by the door, the door,

Down on your knees on floor, on floor,

The Lord of all you come to adore,

On Christmas Day in the morning.

This, Christian men, is your inn, your inn,

Brothers in arms one kin, one kin,

Your host a Babe born without sin

On Christmas Day in the morning.

Sing you good will to men, to men,

Glory to God in the Highest, and then

Praise to the Babe in Bethlehem

On Christmas Day in the morning.

Christmas 1925

The CAROL of the THREE BROTHERS

"Come with me little brothers three

And though the wind blows chill

And dark the night, the Star burns bright

Over Bethlehem's hill.

"The path is rough with splintered stones

And heavy lies the snow,

But here a latch and 'neath the thatch

A lamp swings to and fro."

"Open the door and peep within

Brother, what do you see?"

"An ass asleep, and an ox asleep,

All dreaming peacefully."

"Brother of mine what see you here

At opening of the door?"

"A man, a maid, who unafraid

Kneel on the sanded floor."

"Brother so small look through the chink,

What do you find, oh, say?"

"A Child I see, who smiles at me

From out of a bed of hay."

"What brought you, brother, to the Child?"

"A crown of holly, bright;"

"A crown of thorn, shall His head adorn;

Holly He wears to-night."

"Have you a gift, oh! brother, dear?"

"A silver reed I bring,"

"At passion-tide, it pierced His side

Now a scepter for a King."

"What bring you Him, brother so small?"

"A bunch of hyssop wild;"

"A drink of gall, for the Lord of all;

Now a posy for a Child."

"Sleep little brothers, oh, sleep sound;

Sleep till the breaking dawn;

Ox, ass and sheep a vigil keep

To-night a Child is born."

Christmas 1926

A LULLABY CAROL

Rap softly on the door, then open it wide;

What shall we find if we peep inside?

A Baby in the hay, a Father near by

A Mother who sings a child's lullaby.

Little Child Jesus, Jesus dear Child,

Mary, His Mother ('twas Mary who smiled),

Joseph, dear Father, see we kneel here,

Tell us, oh tell us, may we draw near?

The wind blows so cold, the stable is warm,

Give shelter to-night, out of the storm,

The road is so dark, the way is so drear,

Our bodies are weary, our hearts full of fear.

Cover us, Mary, with fresh scented hay,

And sing us to sleep, and Saint Joseph lay

Kind hands in blessing, for children we are,

Lonely and homeless, who followed a star.

Little Child Jesus, greet with a smile

Poor little brothers, who all the long while

Dreamed of His love, of His warmth and His light,

In the low raftered stable, out of the night.

Here, here is comfort for one and for all,

Warmth in the manger, food in the stall,

Mary and Joseph a night watch to keep

Over tired children who dreamless shall sleep.

Christmas 1927

GOLD, FRANKINCENSE and MYRRH

Three Kings rode from East and West,

Caspar, Balthazar and Melchior,

They followed a star that blazed o'erhead

Miles upon miles had they been led

To see a Child in the lowly bed,

As a swallow in a nest.

Three Kings spoke as they rode their way,

Caspar, Balthazar and Melchior,

"Are the caskets safe that hide the gold,

Incense and myrrh; do the frail clasps hold?

For these in Solomon's days were old,

Usage and rust betray."

"The locks are sound, the gifts secure,

Caspar, Balthazar and Melchior,

Sealed were they in a land afar

When ye went forth to follow a star,

To find the greatest of things that are,

The Son of a Virgin pure.

Mary will know the gifts you bring,

Caspar, Balthazar and Melchior,

Mary will keep your gold apart,

Mary who did keep* things in her heart,

Things that gladden and things that smart;

Will hold these for a King."

The Three Kings answered, "Yes, we bear,

Caspar, Balthazar and Melchior,

Gold for a King, incense for Priest,

Myrrh for a death, for that at least

Three Kings journeyed out of the East

To see a stable bare.

Ah, Mary! take the gifts we lay,

Caspar, Balthazar and Melchior.

Low at His feet, His tiny feet

That shall walk the plain, the sea, the street;"

And Mary smiled, with a smile so sweet,

At the young Child in the hay.

Christmas card says "deep" but one suspects this is a typo.—Ed.

Christmas 1928

WHAT MANNER of SALUTATION?

How shall we greet Thee

Babe of the morning?

How to salute Thee

At the day's dawning?

King of Eternity,

Encircled in space;

What salutation,

What tribute, what grace,

From Thy children kneeling

In day's faintest light?

Who wandered to find Thee

Through the dark night;

What doest Thou ask of us?

A throne for a King?

A scepter, a crown?

Ah, nothing we bring.

Red robes for a Priest,

Insignia of power?

The mitre, the staff,

These for Thy dower?

God for the Victor?

Trumpet and banner?

Thus to salute Thee

After this manner?

Are we not troubled

Like Mary in mind,

At what salutation

Our poor hearts can find?

What may a Child ask?

A smile, a soft touch;

Warm arms for cradle,

So little—so much.

Thy Mother gave these,*

While angels attendant,

Whispered unthinkable

Glory resplendent.

We caught at the vision,

One moment of sight;

The day's salutation,

A flame, after night.

* Another version adds these lines here:

Thy Mother gave these;

Gave to God without fear.

To her salutation

Is added—a tear.

Christmas 1929

SED EX DEO NATI SUNT

(But Are Born of God, see John 1:13—Ed.)

God, in an idle mood one day

Fashioned His image out of clay,

And as He turned the lovely head,

"I will put Reason there," He said.

And whispered as He set the eyes,

"Be very wise, be very wise."

And as He formed the tender lips

With beauty-feeling finger tips,

"Be open, Ephphatha," He cried,

"Tell of My glory, far and wide."

And softly as the ears He laid, said

"Be unafraid, be unafraid."

And swiftly as the body grew,

The hands within His own He drew,

"I will place Power here," and pressed

The upturned palms to East and West;

"I give him freedom of the will,

For good or ill, for good or ill."

The slender feet He firmly made

One over other gently laid;

"The feet of him who brings good news

Bathed in the cool of mountain dews,

Earth shall they walk and shall not stray;

The narrow way, the narrow way."

The Father said, "This is my Son,"

And breathed the breath of life thereon.

"Him, first and last of all things made

Angels shall worship;" and He bade

Michael, Gabriel, Uriel stand

On either hand, on either hand.

When God had made the perfect Man,

The Word with Him ere worlds began,

There rushed the flaming fires of heaven

Athwart the mighty planets seven

And fell in showers of starry mirth

His Peace on earth, His Peace on earth.

Christmas 1930

The CRADLE of the WINDS

University of Notre Dame, Indiana, USA

From frozen ice lands blows the wind of the North,

The cold wind of danger, wild wind of wrath,

Mystery wind, sing loud, sing deep,

Sing to a Babe that is lying asleep,

  Sing loud, sing deep;

Blow wind, blow through the stable door,

Scatter the dead leaves over the floor.

Mary, fold closer the covering hay;

Wind of the North that comes this way,

Is quick to harden, quick to slay

  Pray, Mary Pray.

From the high mountains blows the winds of the East,

The dry wind of menace, anger released;

Magical wind, sing low, sing high,

Sing to an ass that is standing by,

  Sing low, sing high.

Blow wind, blow through the narrow chink,

Ox, ass, and sheep may tremble and shrink

Mary, wait for the sign of day;

Wind of the East that comes this way,

Ready for battle, ready to flay;

  Pray, Mary pray.

From golden deserts blows the wind of the South,

Wind of the spices, a kiss on the mouth;

Whispering wind, sing up, sing down,

Sing to a Maid, that shall wear a crown,

  Sing up, sing down.

Blow wind, blow through the broken rafter,

Fill the pitiful stable with laughter,

Gently blow where Angels play;

Wind of the South that comes this way

Ever to wander, never to stay.

  Pray, Mary pray.

From the deep forest blows the wind of the West,

Wind of the Spirit, wind of the Quest,

O changing wind, sing shine, sing rain,

Sing to a world that is born again,

  Sing shine, sing rain;

Breathe, softly breathe and lift the hair

Of the Child that lies in slumber there,

Wind so gracious, wind so gay,

Wind of the West that comes this way,

Lightly let His cradle sway,

   Pray, Mary pray.

He holds the great winds in His helpless hand

From forest and desert, mountain and land,

The octave notes from near and far

Call to the men who follow a Star

   From near, from far;

Winds shake the bells in the high church steeple,

Summon the king, the priest and the people,

Each in his ordained array,

To holy night, to holy day;

The winds of God have come this way.

   Pray, Mary pray.

Christmas 1931

THE LOWLY GIFTS

How deep the snow, how cruel the wind,

Cold is the stone of the stable wall;

"What shall we do," said Ox to Ass,

"To warm the Lord of all?"

"Here is my wool," said poor little Lamb,

"To weave Him a covering rare;

Fold it around the small hands and feet;

Let me the winter bear."

"Nay," said the Ox, "Mother, here is my hide,

To make Him a jerkin and shoes;

Though worn by the yoke, strong will they prove;

Mary, do not refuse."

"And what can I give?" said old Brother Ass,

"Despised and ill-treated of men;

Nought but my back to carry Him safe

To Egypt from Bethlehem."

Answered Our Lady, "Dear creatures all,

These gifts for the Baby Christ?

The wool shall weave Him the seamless robe

When the Lamb is sacrificed.

And the shoes for Him who brings good news;

Or a scourge of leathern thong

That shall cut the flesh of my little Son

In that day of bitter wrong.

And the back of an Ass shall be marked

In that moment of utter loss,

With the sign of shame and dishonour:

The sign of a Cross."

"Alas—woe is me," said Ox unto Ass;

"Alas," said the trembling Sheep,

"Yet take my fleece for His coverlet

That quietly He may sleep."

"And my hide for His shoes," said friend Ox;

"For tender are children's feet,

Not to be dashed against the stones

Of the rough, paved street."

"And my back to carry the burden

That none but I can bear,"

Said proud Ass to his companions

In the stable there.

Christmas 1932

AND IT WAS WINTER

The curtain of sky hangs a white cloud above,

Soft is the ground and living the grass,

Noisy the birds and swaying the trees,

And light are the feet that pass and repass;

And a whisper abroad, a quiver of wing;

Surely the Child will come with the spring.

But no Child plays with the daffodils gold,

And greener the grass in meadow and glade;

High summer burns, a magnificent sun,

Quickening and ripening the ear in the blade;

Cry aloud every bird, every river that flows,

Lovely the Child that comes with the rose.

Faded the rose that no Child has plucked,

Red gold the beech tree, and purple the vine—

Autumn largesse flung o'er orchard and field

With tangle of berry and eglantine;

Gather the harvest, bind up the sheaf,

The Child will come with the fall of the leaf.

No Child has gathered the leaves as they fall;

Darker the sky, where no twitter of bird

Breaks the deep brooding snow in the air;

Deep sleep in the wood, no fledgling has stirred;

Grey heaven above and grey earth below;

Shall a Babe be born with the fall of the snow?

The silence is broken; the bleat of a lamb,

Soft falls the breathing and lowing of kine,

Footsteps of shepherds, the trumpet of kings

Thunder of Angels—in Heaven a sign;

The Nativity Star, the herald of birth:

Goodwill towards men and peace upon earth.

In Paradise sing, angelical choir,

Shepherds pipe low to the ear of a Maid,

Proclaim, oh wise Men, the King of all kings

As sleeping, the Child in the manger is laid;

Tell the whole earth, bear the news far and wide

Of a Babe in the stable at Christmas tide.

Christmas 1933

LUX MUNDI

(The Light of the World)

Deep darkness broods over Bethlehem;

Call for a light—call for a light,

Flood with the crimson of Cherubim

The quivering shadows of night.

Wonder red of Cherubim wings

Nothing can dim—nothing can dim,

And blue, the blue of the firmament,

Is the sapphire of Seraphim.

Fill the cave with the purple of kings,

For gold we cry—for gold we cry;

And the Star in the East climbs slowly

The stairway of the sky.

Blue and red and gold for His crown;

What for His feet—what for His feet?

The guarded flames of the Magi's lamps

Gleam softly across the street.

Light from bejeweled Eastern lands

They bring with them—they bring with them,

With lantern in hand; low kneeling

Come the Shepherds of Bethlehem.

Tiny tapers through panes of horn

Burn as a fire—burn as a fire,

But Mary kindles a candle set

In a corner of the byre.

This is the Light—true Light that comes

Unto His own—unto His own,

And darkness hath not comprehended

The King on a manger throne.

But they who know and received Him

Outcast and poor—outcast and poor,

And children with bright eyes of wonder

Lift up the latch of the door.

With singing and laughter they enter

(Bend low the head—bend low the head)

The light that shines in the darkness

Is the candle by His bed.

Christmas 1934

IN COELO ET TERRA

(In Heaven and Earth)

King Herod's hall is hung with curtains of pure gold,

King Jesus has bare boards to keep out the cold;

Crimson carpets glow on Herod's palace floor,

But dead leaves are drifting through the stable door.

King Herod has a great couch draped in satin red,

Baby Jesus slumbers with straw for His bed;

The couch has a covering of softest feather down,

Little King Jesus has His Mother's blue gown.

Round King Herod's throne are guests of high degree,

Princes and courtiers all bending low the knee;

Ox, ass and sheep, Child Jesus's servants stand

One on His left and two at His right hand.

To proud Herod's palace come kings of every land,

From Babylon and Tarshish, from Rome and Samarkand;

In the lowly outhouse shepherds and Wise Men pray

To the young Child Jesus asleep in the hay.

From tall torches flash a thousand tongues of flame,

To the glory of Rome and great King Herod's name;

In the midnight sky, blinding wonder released,

Burns in lonely splendour His Star in the East.

In King Herod's chamber, the courtly singers sing

To sackbut and psaltery, to dulcimer and string;

Above the mean stable, to the angelic lyre,

Thunders the Gloria of the heavenly choir.

Christmas 1937

NOW IS OUR SALVATION

NEARER THAN WE BELIEVED

Remote, remote, in distance, space and time

In God's foreknowledge lies the fate of man;

Made in His image, blinded and afraid

Of Death so long, and Life so short a span.

"Look to the hills," he cries, "whence cometh help;"

Silent the hills, immovable the rock,

Save where some Shepherds in the deepening night

Move with slow footsteps onward with their flock.

How can he count the gathering of the stars

The million candles of the Milky Way?

Numbers are nothing, see the Planet's flame

That guides the Wise Men with so bright a ray.

Heartrending is the call of man to God,

Is there no answer to his loud lament?

Hark! the glad music of an Angel choir

Down rushing from the boundless firmament.

So near, so near, beloved, Salvation lies,

Oh fearful man, stretch out thy trembling hand

And touch the Child that shelters in a cave,

And with the Shepherds and the Wise Men, stand

Before thy Maker, mortal man, and heed;

Distance nor space nor time will God renew;

Here is the place, the Word, the appointed hour,

Now is Salvation nearer than we knew.

These next two poems are most likely Christmas card poems. Published by Ashdown Ltd, London in 1954 as a musical score, music by Eva Fovargue, permission to use words given by Miss D.E. Collins. —Ed.

THE KINGS OF OLD

The Kings of old came to Thy bed.

Bringing their gifts of gold,

Incense and myrrh with homage meet,

To the Babe content with hay so sweet,

Safe from the cruel cold.

The Shepherds came to Thy mean bed

Journeying from afar,

Prayer in their hearts, and love that cries

For very joy to the Child

Who lies a-smiling at a star.

And we who come to Thy poor bed,

What gifts can we afford?

Incense has Thou and bitter myrrh,

Our gold, our prayers.

Thy worshippers lay at Thy feet, a sword.

HERE IS THE LITTLE DOOR

Here is the little door, lift up the latch, O lift!

We need not wander more but enter with our gift;

Our gift of finest gold,

Gold that was never bought or sold;

Myrrh to be strewn about His bed;

Incense in clouds about His head;

All for the Child that stirs not in His sleep,

But holy slumber holds with ass and sheep.

Bend low about His bed, for each He has a gift,

See how His eyes awake, lift up your hands, O lift!

For gold, He gives a keen-edged sword

(Defend with it Thy little Lord!)

For incense, smoke of battle red

Myrrh for the honoured happy dead;

Gifts for His children, terrible and sweet,

Touched by such tiny hands and Oh such tiny feet.

[Music for Here is the Little Door *by Herbert Howells (1892-1983)—Ed.]*

APPENDIX

A Brief Explanation of Heraldry
by Peter J. Floriani, PhD

Heraldry is the name for a very special branch of art: the art of a coat of arms. But heraldry can also be called a science since it has very definite rules, unlike most other kinds of art. There are two main reasons for this. First, heraldry deals with family and inheritance - a coat of arms can tell the history of its owner. Second, a coat of arms always has a precise description called a blazon which tells exactly what is on the shield: every item, its color, and its placement are spelled out using a technical language, almost as special as the graphical languages used in computing or engineering.

Why are there coats of arms anyway? Simply for identification. You've seen those big motorcycle helmets which conceal the driver's face - in the Middle Ages, the knights also used helmets which hid their faces. So they decided to paint their shields with bright colors, so their teammates would know who's who—just like a football team wears colored jerseys. It was also handy since not everyone could read - so nametags or numbers—like in football—wouldn't be any help; but it was very easy to spot the color codes, even from a good distance. As this idea caught on, the knights began using their colors and arms on all sorts of things, even their clothes. But the usual way of showing one's arms is on a shield, which is drawn as a sort of triangular thing, like a garden spade.

The herald was the person who heralded—or announced—a guest. He could read the arms, and in Frances Chesterton's plays, he recited the blazon of the shield, then stated the name or title of that person.

The blazon is the technical language which describes the shield. In general all the colors are bright—so they can be seen from a good distance away. There were just six colors used, and they used old words to name them:

Two "metals":

> Or   gold or yellow
> Argent silver or white

Four "tinctures":

> Gules red
> Azure blue
> Vert   green
> Sable black

They sometimes used purple and orange, but not very often. Also, everyone knew that certain combinations were easy to see, and others weren't; this was so important it became one of the few rules there are: Never put metal upon metal, or tincture upon tincture.

The other words in the blazon tell the artist what to draw, and where to draw it.

There are many other things to tell about how to design a coat of arms, and how to write its blazon, and about its history—but for our purpose we shall just add one brief comment: when you design your own, keep it simple and bright, remembering its purpose is to identify you. Now, let's consider the six blazons from the play.

The Six Blazons for the Characters in "The Children's Crusade."

1. Field Or, Lion Rampant Sable, Godfrey de Bouillon.
The shield is gold/yellow, and the black lion faces left—he is rampant as if he was fighting.

2. Field Gules, Three Lions Passant Or, The King of England. The shield is red, and there are three gold/yellow lions lying down.

Note that this is a Royal emblem in England and respected as a national symbol, just like we respect the flag.

3. Field Argent, Chevron Gules, Three Mullets of the Field. The Queen of England.

The shield is silver/white; on it is a red chevron, which is a V-shape, pointing upwards; you may know this word from a gasoline company, or from the military. Upon the chevron are three white stars.

4. Cross Patè, Sable, Field Argent, The Knight Templar.

The shield is silver/white; on it is a black cross with curved arms. There are all sorts of crosses used in heraldry.

5. Field Azure, Three Fleur de Lys Or, The King of France.

The shield is blue; on it are three gold fleur de lys—these are often considered to be stylized representations of a lily-flower. These were an official symbol when France was a kingdom.

6. Part-per-Pale, Dexter Field Azure, Seme of Fleur de Lys Or, Sinister Field Argent Castle Gules, Tancred of Tiberias.

The shield is divided vertically. In order to understand the rest, you have to know that the blazon is based on the shield-bearer's hands, not the way we see it. So that means the dexter half—dexter is Latin for right—is the half of the shield on the shield-bearer's right—which appears on our left. And sinister side, which means left in Latin, is on our right. That is why the left half is blue, and the right half is silver/white. The left half is strewn with gold fleur-de-lys symbols, and the right half bears a red castle.

The actors and stage crew should make their own shields. They should be made by hand—and use the brightest colors—gold and silver are preferred, but yellow and white are acceptable if not otherwise available.

Reference: *Heraldry* by Julian Franklyn, 1965.

***

NOTE:
The editor of this book would very much be interested to know if any group, organization or family puts on one of these plays of Frances Chesterton's. Please send pictures, video clips, links or any newspaper clippings to: nancycbrown47@gmail.com.

The editor is also very interested in finding more of Frances Chesterton's poetry. If you have any information, please email. Thank you.

Frances Alice Blogg Chesterton—A Brief Timeline

Chronology

1869	June 28th—Frances Alice Blogg is born
1871	Her brother George Alfred Knollys is born
1872	Her sister Ethel is born
1873	Her sister Helen is born
1874	Gilbert Keith Chesterton is born
1875	Helen dies
1876	Her sister Gertrude is born
1878	Her father called to active service
1881	Boards at German School in London with Ethel
1883	Father's death
1891	Employed variously as secretary or tutor
1896	Begins work at P.N.E.U. as secretary
1896	Meets Gilbert Keith Chesterton
1898	Becomes engaged
1899	Gertrude's accidental death
1900	GKC's first two books published, *The Wild Knight* and *Greybeards at Play*

1901	Marriage to G.K. Chesterton, sets up house in Kensington for a few months
1901	Move to 48 Overstrand Mansions, Battersea, London
1904	Gilbert and Frances meet Fr. John O'Connor
1908	George Knollys commits suicide
1908	Operation to improve fertility
1909	Move to Beaconsfield
1909	Accepts the fact that she cannot bear children
1911	Ballad of the White Horse published—dedicated to Frances
1911	Chesterton quote book published, selections by Frances
1912-13	Marconi Scandal
1914-15	GKC's major illness, almost dies
1917	GKC's brother Cecil marries Ada Eliza Jones (who uses the pen name John Keith Prothero, and is known by all as "Keith")
1918	Cecil dies
1919	Palestine tour
1920	Italy tour
1921	United States tour
1922	GKC's father dies
1922	GKC converts to Roman Catholicism

1922   Writes the play *The Children's Crusade* and Geoffrey Shaw sets "Crusader's Carol," aka "The Shepherds Found Thee by Night" to music

1922   *How Far Is It To Bethlehem?* is published by Novello & Co as musical score

1923   *The Shepherds Found Thee by Night*—is published by Novello & Co.

1924   *The Children's Crusade, Sir Cleges, The Christmas Gift Three Plays for Children* is published by Samuel French

1925   *Piers Plowman's Pilgrimage* is published by Samuel French

1926   25th Wedding Anniversary

1926   Converts to Roman Catholicism

1926   Dorothy Collins is hired as GKC's new secretary

1927   Poland trip

1929   Rome trip

1930-31 United States again, and Canada

1932   GKC begins radio talks on the BBC

1932   Dorothy Collins converts to Roman Catholicism

1933   GKC's mother dies. Frances's mother dies.

1934   Rome again

1935   France and Italy

1935   GKC nominated for the Nobel Prize for Literature

1936   Reviews *I Lived In a Slum* by Ada Chesterton in G.K.'s Weekly

1936   Lourdes and Lisieux, France

1936   GKC dies

1936   Frances visits cousins in Germany

1937   Frances diagnosed with cancer

1938   December 12th—Frances dies

List of Known Published Works of Frances Chesterton

According to Maisie Ward (G.K. Chesterton, page 665) Frances's poetry was published in *"The Observer, The Sunday Times, The Daily Chronicle, The Westminster Gazette* and *The New Witness."* Not all of these have been found yet.

1900	Parents' Review	Volume XI The Open Road (as Frances Blogg)
1901	Parents' Review	Volume XII P.N.E.U. Natural History Clubs (as F. Blogg)
1913	Ashburton Guardian	March 27, The Small Dreams
1918	Stainer & Bell	Here Is the Little Door (Lyrics)
1921	MacMilliam & Co.	*To Felicity Who Calls Me Mary* in a book of English Verse on Infancy & Childhood

1922	Novello & Co.	How Far Is It To Bethlehem? (Lyrics)
1923	Novello & Co.	The Musical Times (Vol. 64, No 97)
		The Shepherds Found Thee by Night (aka The Crusader's Carol) (Lyrics)
1924	Samuel French, Ltd.	*The Children's Crusade, Sir Cleges, The Christmas Gift: Three Plays for Children*
1924	Houghton Mifflin	The poem, How Far Is It To Bethlehem? is reprinted in *The Magic Carpet: Poems for Travelers*, selected by Mrs. Waldo Richards, pg 462
1925	Samuel French, Ltd.	*Piers Plowman's Pilgrimage: A Morality Play*
1928	Oxford University Press *The Oxford Book of Carols*	How Far Is It To Bethlehem? (originally Percy Dearmer, et al., eds., composed in 1917 included on Christmas card to friends that year)
1929	Evening Post	December 17, A Nativity Song (aka How Far is it to Bethlehem? aka Children's Song of the Nativity)
1934	Sheed & Ward	Gospel Rhymes, page 9 *The Lowly Gifts*

| 1937 | The Observer | October 3, <u>Must We Forever Say a Long Farewell</u> |
| 1938 | UK Guardian | November 27, <u>Things to Think About</u> |

Suggested Reading

G.K. Chesterton: A Centenary Appraisal Edited by John Sullivan. Harper & Row, 1974

The Collected Works of G.K. Chesterton, Ignatius Press, all volumes.

Basil Howe: A Story of Young Love, introduced by Denis Conlon. New City London, 2001.

Wisdom and Innocence: A Life of G.K. Chesterton, Pearce, Joseph. Ignatius Press: San Francisco, 1996.

Father Vincent McNabb, O.P.: Portrait of a Great Dominican, Ferdinand Valentine, O.P., Newman Press, Maryland, 1955.

Gilbert Keith Chesterton, Maisie Ward, Sheed & Ward, New York, 1943.

Return to Chesterton, Maisie Ward, Sheed & Ward, New York, 1952.

Chesterton and the Romance of Orthodoxy: The Making of GKC 1874-1908, William Oddie, Oxford University Press, Oxford, 2008.

The Elusive Father Brown: The Life of Mgr. John O'Connor, Julia Smith, Gracewing, Herefordshire, 2010.

The Children's Crusade, Sir Cleges, The Christmas Gift: Three Plays for Children, Frances Chesterton, Samuel French, Ltd. London,1924.

Piers Plowman's Pilgrimage: A Morality Play Frances Chesterton, Samuel French, Ltd. London,1925.

Chesterton as Seen by His Contemporaries, Cyril Clemens, Gordon Press, New York, 1972.

Gilbert Magazine, published by The American Chesterton Society

Conrad Noel: An Autobiography, Conrad Noel, J.M. Dent & Sons Ltd., London, 1945

The Eye of the Beholder, Lance Sieveking, Hulton Press, London, 1957.

Hilaire Belloc: A Biography, A.N. Wilson, New York: Atheneum Books, 1984.

The Outline of Sanity : A Biography of G.K. Chesterton, Alzina Stone Dale, 1982, Grand Rapids, Mich. : Eerdmans

G.K. Chesterton; A Biography, Dudley Barker, 1973, New York, Stein and Day

The Chestertons, Mrs. Cecil Chesterton, London : Chapman & Hall, 1941.

G.K. Chesterton: A Biography, Ian Ker, Oxford University Press, 2011.

Index to the Poems (Poem Titles)

Index to First lines

Is there a sound, a sound as sweet   229

It was very late, and very cold   324

King Herod's hall is hung with curtains of pure gold   359

Last night Our Lady whispered to her Son   273

Little Child Jesus, asleep in the Manger   296

Mid all the noises of the world I know   300

Must we forever say a long farewell   308

My heart leaps with the sunrise   244

My soul went groping all the past years through   248

No terror can touch them   234

O where is the fearful wild hair   200

Of Island Dreams of palm and coral reef and spice   206

Of your charity, pray for his soul   237

Oh golden leaves of London, dancing in the sun   291

On this wide sofa where I lie   242

Our Lady, ours no longer, we have left her and she   274

Our tale is told, our play is done   283

Poppies have reared their haunting heads   280

Rap softly on the door, then open it wide   337

Remote, remote, in distance, space, and time   361

Sometimes my soul is sick for alien skies   254

General Index

ABOUT THE EDITOR

Nancy Carpentier Brown is a wife and a retired veteran homeschool mother. Brown is on staff and Media Manager for The American Chesterton Society, managing the Facebook Fan Page, Twitter, Pinterest and YouTube channel, as well as blogging at chesterton.org. In addition, she creates and hosts the podcast Uncommon Sense: The Official Podcast of the American Chesterton Society. Mrs. Brown is also a regular columnist for Gilbert Magazine, and has written for numerous other publications. She is on the editorial board of *mater et magister*, the Catholic Homeschooling Magazine. Brown teaches at Homeschool Connections.

Brown's books include *The Father Brown Reader: Stories from Chesterton*, *The Father Brown Reader 2: More Stories from Chesterton*, *Chesterton's The Blue Cross: Study Edition*, *A Study Guide for G. K. Chesterton's St. Francis of Assisi*; and *The Mystery of Harry Potter: A Catholic Family Guide* (published by Our Sunday Visitor). Brown is the winner of the Kilby Research Grant for her work on Frances A. Chesterton, wife of G.K. Chesterton.

http://chesterton.org

http://mrsnancybrown.blogspot.com/

http://www.twitter.com/amchestertonsoc

http://www.youtube.com/AmCHESTERTONsoc

http://www.facebook.com/AmericanChestertonSociety

http://www.facebook.com/UncommonSensePodcast

uncommonsensepodcast@gmail.com

http://pinterest.com/amchestertonsoc

http://homeschoolconnectionsonline.com/

Printed in Great Britain
by Amazon